SINK OR SWIM

GET YOUR DEGREE WITHOUT DROWNING IN DEBT

SINK OR SWIM

SARAH DEVEAU

Foreword by Will Ferguson

THE DUNDURN GROUP
TORONTO · OXFORD

Copy-Editor: Artemis Creative Consulting
Design: Jennifer Scott
Printer: Transcontinental

National Library of Canada Cataloguing in Publication Data

Deveau, Sarah
  Sink or swim : get your degree without drowning in debt / Sarah Deveau.

Includes bibliographical references.
ISBN 1-55002-449-3

1. College students--Canada--Finance, Personal. I. Title.

HG179.D442 2003   332.024'375   C2003-901651-X

1   2   3   4   5   07   06   05   04   03

 **Canada**

THE CANADA COUNCIL | LE CONSEIL DES ARTS
FOR THE ARTS | DU CANADA
SINCE 1957 | DEPUIS 1957

ONTARIO ARTS COUNCIL
CONSEIL DES ARTS DE L'ONTARIO

We acknowledge the support of the **Canada Council for the Arts** and the **Ontario Arts Council** for our publishing program. We also acknowledge the financial support of the **Government of Canada** through the **Book Publishing Industry Development Program** and **The Association for the Export of Canadian Books**, and the **Government of Ontario** through the **Ontario Book Publishers Tax Credit** program, and the **Ontario Media Development Corporation's Ontario Book Initiative.**

Care has been taken to trace the ownership of copyright material used in this book. The author and the publisher welcome any information enabling them to rectify any references or credit in subsequent editions.

                                                    J. Kirk Howard, President

Printed and bound in Canada.⊛
Printed on recycled paper.
www.dundurn.com

Dundurn Press
8 Market Street
Suite 200
Toronto, Ontario, Canada
M5E 1M6

Dundurn Press
73 Lime Walk
Headington, Oxford,
England
OX3 7AD

Dundurn Press
2250 Military Road
Tonawanda NY
U.S.A. 14150

SINK OR SWIM

Acknowledgements

I'd like to thank everyone at The Dundurn Group for your support, guidance, and above all, your patience!

There have been many influential people in my life: Gail White, Will Ferguson, Mike Dempster, and Brent Kawchuk. You are all individuals I look to for guidance and advice. Your drive, determination, and success have inspired and challenged me – thank you for your words of encouragement over the years.

A big thanks to my friends and family who always believed in me, even when I had second thoughts! Thank you Keith, Russ, Leo, Aline, Edith, Roman, Justin, Sarah, Kevin, Susan, Jesse, Amber, and Maccall.

And finally, thank you to the many students, graduates, and experts who contributed their experiences and ideas to this book.

Table of Contents

Foreword

When I first met Sarah Deveau she was in her final year of university. She was about to leave the warm, fuzzy world of academia and be thrown into that arena of hardknocks otherwise known as "the real world," and yet far from being distressed, she seemed oddly upbeat. Optimistic, even. Clearly, poor Sarah was unprepared for what was coming. It was like seeing a puppy scamper about on a busy railway crossing with a freight train bearing down.

"Ah, yes," I said, with a knowing, yet saintly smile (the type that comes only with the wisdom of years).

> Your schooldays are coming to a close, the dreamy reverie is over. Now comes the cold splash of water: crippling debt, scant prospects, a groaning financial burden that would make even Atlas feel—

"But I don't have any real debts," she said, sweetly, in much the same way that a deluded lunatic might say, "Oh, no, gravity doesn't apply to me."

"Come on," I said. "By now you must be staggering under the weight of your monetary obligations and facing a bleak future peppered with stern letters from cruel bank lenders demanding that you start coughing up the interest on the government-sponsored largesse that they so kindly approved way back when you were..." My voice trailed off as I realized, to my stunned amazement, *that she was serious.*

Get this. Sarah Deveau and her husband have, between the two of them, completed more than twelve years of post-secondary education. Total debt? Just $6,000.

There was obviously some mistake. "Surely you mean, $60,000 for the two of you?"

Nope.

"Ah," I said with a saccharine smile. "Rich parents. Must be nice."

Nope. No wealthy familial connections. No trust fund. No credit cards. Sarah had simply managed her money smartly, and in doing so had succeeded in becoming that most remarkable of creatures: the debt-free graduate.

I had heard rumours of such a thing; urban legends, really, of power-point preppies who had taken their student loans and invested them with such uncanny business acumen that they were able to live off the interest alone. But these investment bankers passing themselves off as students were, I suspect, works of wishful fiction.

After all, I had invested my student loan as well – mainly in empties and pizza boxes – but you didn't see me turning a profit. (The return on beer bottles is shockingly low.)

I graduated from university with a massive debt, one so heavy I spent the next five years working overseas just to pay it off. It wasn't a pleasurable experience, going from the 'fun poverty' of being a student to the 'very real and not-so-fun poverty' of being a recent university graduate. I flailed about for years after I graduated, dog-paddling like mad, trying desperately to keep my head above water. What I wouldn't have given for a copy of *Sink or Swim.*

This is a remarkable book. It provides a wealth of no-nonsense, practical advice on everything from accommodation to transportation, from funding to food. It even contains tips on "getting laid on a budget." (And oh, how I could have used that back in my debt-ridden dorm days!)

Indeed. If only I could FedEx a copy of this book to myself at age nineteen, back when I was just about to leap into the deep end of the pool, headfirst. It would have provided a much-needed life preserver. Sink or swim? The choice is yours.

Will Ferguson
February 2003

willferguson.ca

Introduction

Greetings Planet Education

I first conceived of the idea for this book in my last year of university. After a few years of plugging along with no student loans, I was facing tuition, wedding bills, and I desperately wanted a car. I decided to take out a student loan, and was complaining to a friend about the process. She was shocked. Not because of the size of the loan, but because my husband Keith (remember that name, he'll feature often in our misadventures in student financing) and I had managed to get into our last years of university without student loans. I hadn't really thought much of it until I started talking to other students about their debt load. I learned that most of my classmates had student loans, carried credit cards with enormous balances, or relied on lines of credit or personal bank loans to pay tuition and living expenses. I began to think about all the decisions we had made before and during university that got us where we were – the big decisions, the little ones, the right ones, and the wrong ones.

Who am I to tell you what to do?

Born in Dartmouth, Nova Scotia, I spent my childhood in the

Maritimes, dreaming of going to Dalhousie University and becoming a lawyer. My father was a bricklayer, my mother a secretary, and when I was eleven we followed the exodus of labourers heading west and moved to Hamilton, Ontario. I attended junior high in Hamilton, and fell in love with a cute blonde boy named Jamie, but more important-ly, with the idea of attending Ryerson University. In the end, Jamie and I didn't work out, and neither did my dream of studying journalism.

On my fifteenth birthday my parents announced that not only would they be getting a divorce, but that my younger brother and I would be moving with mom to Calgary, Alberta. I attended Bishop Carroll High School in Calgary, and began writing for the *Calgary Herald*, as well as my school newspaper.

By the time I entered grade twelve, I still wanted to go to Ryerson, but the application deadline was looming. I couldn't figure out how I would pay for the tuition and living away from home. Keith and I had been dating for two years, and I didn't want a long distance relation-ship. So I looked at the local schools, and chose the University of Calgary. It had a great Communications program, it was close to home, and Keith was already attending. I applied and was accepted, despite my pathetic marks in Math and Biology.

I began university the fall after finishing high school. In the five years it took to get my bachelor's degree in Communications and Culture, with a major in Communications Studies and minor in Canadian Studies, I worked twelve different jobs (my friends would always ask me to write their resignation letters – I was good at it!). Some of those jobs were full-time summer positions, while others were part-time for as little as a single semester. Keith received his B.A. in Actuarial Science after seven years at the U of C. We lived at home for the first few years of school. Keith had an '85 Escort, affectionately nicknamed our Piece of Shit car, or POS for short. In my fourth year of university we decided to move out and get mar-ried. Keith had recently bought a truck, and I was driving the POS. We sold the Escort for cash for the wedding, and I began taking the big blue limo, Calgary Transit, to school and work again. A year later, just a month before graduation, I bought a used Hyundai Accent. Wheels again!

A few months before graduating from university, I began looking for my dream job. I interviewed for more than a dozen positions. Some paid well for tedious work, others offered terrible wages for interesting work. I was offered the ones I decided I didn't want, and the ones I did want, I was always "a close second." Finding a balance between my need for a stimulating position and a wage that would allow me to pay my bills seemed impossible. When I just couldn't find the job I wanted, I turned to freelancing. Working from home, billing a great hourly rate – it seemed like the perfect career. But I missed the social interaction of an office. Worse, the unpaid time required to find clients and administrate the business killed my productivity, and therefore my billable hours. And my Oprah addiction was frightening off friends.

Six months after graduation, I updated my resumé and began pounding the pavement again. I called my contacts, attended networking events, and followed up with a company I had interviewed with and come in "a close second" for their open position. Turns out, they weren't just being nice – they had really considered offering me the position. When I contacted them again, they were just about ready to post a second position and called me in for another round of interviews. Success! I landed the job of Communications Co-ordinator.

So I've been a productive member of society for over a year now. Soon after landing my current job I asked my manager why she chose me for the position. She said it was my obvious skills in organization and multi-tasking, and my ambitiousness – all developed as I struggled to graduate from university without drowning in debt. Decisions I made to pay the bills often turned out to be decisions impacting my resumé in a very positive way.

So that's my story. I'm not ashamed of what I owe, or how much money I've made. Throughout this book I'll talk about the good and bad decisions we made, the debts we incurred, the salaries we made. I graduated from university owing $6,235 in student loans. I owed the bank $8,000 for the car, and for once, my Visa was clear. In the two years since graduation I've paid off the car, paid down the student loans to under $2,000, and now owe the bank an astronomical mortgage. I think I have the topic for my next book.

REALITY CHECK: How-to books are the strangest things. *Retire at Twenty-five.* Sure, if I had bought real estate in the '80s and made 18% interest on my investments, I definitely could retire at twenty-five. Today's reality is thousands of retirees are rejoining the workforce because their portfolios have plummeted. *Find the Unknown Scholarships.* You've just effectively made them very well known scholarships.

Most how-to books ignore what they think of as the exceptions to the rule. In today's world of blended families, divorce, and stock market havoc, exceptions are the rule. Your life will be completely different from anyone else's reading this book. I sincerely hope you'll graduate debt-free, and I'll do my best to help you achieve this. If you can't, don't be discouraged. Your goal and your way of achieving it are as individual as you are, and I will do my best to give you the tools you need, whatever your situation.

I couldn't have written this book without having gone through the process of obtaining, living with, and paying off student loans. My intent is not to give you one perfect way to get out of school debt-free, but to provide you with the tools you need to make the best decisions in terms of financing an education and a future. By reading about my experiences, and those of students in various walks of life across Canada, I hope you'll see that getting a post-secondary education doesn't have to mean incurring an excessive debt load or living in poverty.

One more thing

Getting your education is like swimming across a huge ocean. You can sink to the bottom, overcome by waves of credit cards, student loans, and unchecked consumerism. Or you can swim to the shore, propelled by your commitment, positive choices, and perseverance. If you've decided to swim it won't be easy. Along the way you're going to lose your direction, be pushed under by waves of bad decisions, and confront unforeseeable challenges. But you will emerge on the other side of the ocean, ready to take on even bigger challenges with the strength you've discovered by overcoming this one.

CHAPTER ONE
Welcome to the Worst Years of Your Life

When I started university, I thought, "I'll get through the first year without a loan." After the first year, I landed a summer job that I thought paid well, until I realized I was spending so much money on dress clothes and lunches out that I was really only bringing home minimum wage. I ended up beginning my second year of university without the safety net I had been counting on. Every year was the same: I'd slowly fall into debt while I was in school, and the following summer I'd work to catch up on the debt I had incurred during the school year. I made some wise decisions, but also many bad ones. And at graduation, I still had debt.

What's the big deal about a little debt?

When I entered the working world I had some debt and no stellar job offers. Working freelance was fun, but I could never have managed to make monthly payments on a $20,000 loan, which is the average student debt load. Loan payments come due, whether you're making $7 an hour or $17. And while you may believe it's too early to start thinking about the bigger things in life, such as mortgages, retirement savings, and a fine car, the bank doesn't. Banks are tracking your credit, and won't hesitate to decline your credit application because of a high debt load.

Terra went to the University of Calgary, graduating after four and a half years with a B.A. in Sociology, minor in Management, concentration in Business Organization. Terra never carried a full load of classes; instead she made them up in spring and summer semesters. "My parents really valued education, however, my dad felt that if we wanted to educate ourselves then we should pay for it ourselves. I never applied for scholarships even though I'm sure I would have received some. I applied for both Canada and Alberta loans. In addition, I worked full-time hours bartending my entire university career."

During school Terra took out $12,000 in student loans. "But not for education," she notes. "I purchased a car in my second year, went to Mexico in my third year, and dabbled in the stock market in my fourth year. Generally I had a lot of fun with my money." Ten years later, she's still paying for that long-forgotten fun. Her advice? "Take the loans only if you need them. I really think that working while in school is a great idea. It made me appreciate my education and prepared me for the 'real world.' I didn't have the shock that my friends experienced because I

Bankruptcy

Some students have taken to declaring bankruptcy to avoid repaying their student loans. Simply put, it's financial suicide. Bankruptcy is not the answer. Many people believe bankruptcy means all of your debts are absolved, with no other penalties. If it were that easy, everyone would do it. When you declare bankruptcy you're forced to sell everything you own, except for a few personal possessions — your car, stereo, TV, jewelry, even your classic Nintendo are all going to the bank.

The government is creating initiatives to prevent students from doing this by not absolving student loans unless you've been out of school for at least ten years. And bankruptcy stays on your record for a minimum of five years, undermining any chance you might have had for getting future loans, credit cards, or mortgages.

had always worked and I had treated school like a job, eight hours a day, year round. Working through school made me more marketable, as well. I do wish that I hadn't gotten a loan because I only needed it the first year. It was too easy to get and too easy to spend and very difficult to pay off when life's other priorities took over."

Prepare for your financial future

You may have heard people mention a credit report, or talk about running a credit check. Credit is a key part of an individual's financial history. It can open doors or slam them shut in your face. As a student, you're at a key stage of your financial life, and understanding credit is essential to making it through school the right way.

A credit file is kept by credit reporting agencies; it shows your history of debts. Your credit report is a copy of that file. The credit reporting agency assigns a North American Standard Account Rating to each debt, from R0 to R9. R0 means the debt is approved but too new to rate. R1 means you have been repaying your debt on time, without making overdue payments. R2 is for debts that have been paid late on occasion, and it gets worse from there. R9 is the worst – it's a debt you have never paid that's gone to a collection agency, or one that you tried to move without paying (and yes, avoiding your regular price purchase obligations at Columbia House counts).

A credit report with many R1s is a great report. However, most students will have just one or two notes on their report, and many students won't have any. An empty credit report isn't necessarily good. When it comes time to take out a big loan, if you haven't proven yourself a good borrower, you'll probably be declined. You need to build a credit history before you'll receive any real amount of money from a lender. For instance, if you want to buy a car for $2,000 and you have cash, get a loan instead. Create a separate account for the $2,000 and use that money to pay out the loan in half the time you were supposed to. For the sake of a few bucks interest, you'll be building a good credit history. The catch? You'll be tempted to just take out the loan and blow the money you saved on something else. Don't miss payments or stretch out the repayment so that you pay hundreds in interest.

By understanding how credit works and establishing good credit from the very start, you'll always be aware of your debt load and your credit. Any time you apply for a debt, be it a cell phone contract, a gas card, or a loan, the debt will go into your credit file. The more debt you have, the harder it is to make those monthly payments, and you'll have R5s scattered throughout your report like land mines, ready to destroy any chance you might have had for negotiating a good mortgage rate, or just getting approved for a cell phone.

Credit report

You can request a free copy of your credit file from Equifax Canada Inc. (1-800-465-7166) or Trans Union of Canada (1-800-663-9980). Once you've received it, check it over to ensure it's accurate. Any mistakes should be dealt with immediately, and contact information for corrections is included in the report. If you're unsure of something in the report, set up an appointment at your bank and ask them to explain it to you. It's a service most banks are willing to provide free of charge.

Chris is working for $10 an hour in a construction shop. At twenty-nine, he's spent a few years in college, and a few studying in university. Holding a diploma in Kinesiology, he's had a hard time finding employment in his field. His total student debt was high, but over the years he's whittled it down to about $6,000.

The worst part is that in his experience, the government hasn't been exactly consistent with its payment plan. "It turns out I defaulted on my loans. I had moved a lot, and didn't really keep track of my payments. Not that I'm not sure what they're doing, but the government seems to take money out of my bank account at random. I've tried to buy groceries and my debit card has been declined for insufficient funds. I have terrible credit. If I could do it over again, I wouldn't have treated my loans like free money that I could waste. There's so much responsibility that comes with student loans; it's a lot to handle when you're twenty."

No matter what your situation is, I'm sure you understand the value of graduating with no debt, or at least as little debt as possible. Student loans are not free money – they have to be paid back, with interest. With no guarantee of a good job once you graduate, paying back those loans could set your life plan back years, or derail it altogether.

Two big lies

There are dozens of preconceptions students have about continuing their education that are misguided, half-true, or totally wrong. Here are two common myths you may have come across when talking to your family and friends.

Tuition is too expensive. Yes, tuition has doubled in the past few years. Yes, your parents paid pennies for their education. Yes, in some countries post-secondary education is free. Regardless, none of these things makes any difference right now. Tuition costs are related to the economy and inflation. And the government in Canada is less willing to fund your tuition than it once was.

It's true that the government and society benefit from having a well-educated population. But a Canadian education is basically a government-subsidized education, and there is nothing to prevent you from leaving the country once you have the degree. The government is taking the risk that you'll get your degree and run to the U.S. What do I mean when I say that a Canadian education is subsidized? The government pays most of the cost of your education, to the tune of 70%. Did you realize that students pay for only 30% of their education in Canada? Think about that – is it really such a bad deal? Some student unions claim that the government is only paying 50% of the cost, but only because the government is factoring in research and development costs which don't directly affect student learning.

Did you know international students are required to pay the full cost of their education, and Canadian citizens are not? Keep that in mind when tuition is due. It could be worse. You have so many resources and tools at your disposal that obtaining your education while doing the least damage to your wallet is achievable.

The student life is one big party. The student life is not a non-stop kegger. That would defeat the purpose of your goal – graduating with little or no debt. Yes, students must have time to party. All work and no play will cause more harm than good. While it's true that simply working and studying is stressful and students do need a break once in awhile, hitting the bars every Saturday night and blowing $60 each time is not the best way to go. If you can afford to do this without getting loans, more power to you. However, if you're considering getting a loan because you're running short of money, the loan gods won't accept partying too much as a valid reason for your credit needs.

Later I'll talk about cheap entertainment, but remember that just because it's cheap, doesn't mean it's smart. Inevitably, the students who party the most end up suffering the most. I distinctly remember my partying in the first year of university. There were a handful of my friends who hung out in the campus pub many afternoons or skipped classes to hang out in the food court. They would cut class for "just one more beer, or one more game of pool." Each semester another one bit the dust until finally there weren't enough of us left to drink a pitcher. I was lucky, and learned from the mistakes of others without falling into the "one more beer" abyss. It is a cruel thing for a campus to have a pub, yet they all do. So stay strong! Partying is not the goal of post-secondary, getting an education is.

Tracey is a graduate of Southern Alberta Institute of Technology's Architectural Technologies program. Over three years of schooling she received more than $4,000 in scholarships. Tracey worked during the summer, but spent her spare time playing competitive volleyball during the school year.

Tracey paid for her own tuition, books, and her '89 Corolla while her parents covered her room and board. She lived with relatives and kept her expenses low, using only the money she made in the summer to get by. Tracey is proud to have made it through school without any loans. "Don't take out loans. They give you more than you need and you spend it on stuff you don't need. I admit I didn't have the rowdy college experience, but I had fun enough and was completely free when I graduated. I wish I could've lived with some kick-ass room-mates, but then I wouldn't have been able to keep my funds plentiful due to too much partying."

Getting along with "The Man"

Some students blame the government or their school for raising tuition and forcing them to get student loans to pay for it. They argue that tuition is too high, that it should be lowered or even eliminated. When in school, I agreed. Now that I'm a taxpayer, my views have changed a little. Taxes are incredibly high in Canada already, and for the government to lower tuition fees, it would have to provide post-secondary institutions with more of my tax money. Naturally, this being the government we're talking about, it would continue to fund dumb blonde joke books and dead chicken art. But a discussion about foolish government spending deserves a book of its own.

It is definitely in the best interest of the government to partially fund our education. In 1999, university graduates made up just over 15% of the population but paid close to 35% of the nation's income tax while receiving just 8% of government transfers. In contrast, people with less than a high school education made up 25% of the population but paid just over 10% of all income tax and received over 40% of government transfers.

In the end, our society dictates that the people getting the most benefit should have to pay for the service, and that means students paying for their education. Some students claim that post-secondary education in Canada is only for the wealthy, or is quickly becoming this way. I disagree. Sure, I couldn't afford to move to Toronto and attend Ryerson for four years without getting student loans. It would have cost me well over $20,000 a year. Instead I lived at home for much of university and went to the local school. Keep in mind, your local school is someone else's exotic out-of-province school.

You don't have to be rolling in money to get a degree; you just have to make the smart decisions, even when they are the hard ones. Look for the opportunities that will get you through these two- to five-year programs without bankrupting your future. Reading this book and being interested in your future is a positive step in the right direction. Implementing the ideas contained within this book will be the proof of your willpower and determination, and I know you can make it happen.

Though I'm not certain I want tuition lowered because I'm sure my taxes will go up, I still encourage you to battle the system. Maybe you will change things. But remember when you're holding rallies, writing letters to the government, and protesting at your school that you could be working to pay for tuition! In five years of watching my student union spend my dues fighting for lower tuition, I haven't seen any real change in tuition costs for the better. Couldn't they have put that money into scholarship and financial aid programs?

Some schools have implemented tuition freezes, but they won't last long. What needs to happen is for non-students to get involved in the fight for more government spending on education. Yet there aren't many non-student activists waving the banner of lower tuition. It's really only a concern for students, and they forget about their tuition troubles when they graduate. In the end, many people realize that it's not the government's job to hand out expensively run programs for free, and it's not the government's responsibility to educate the masses past high school.

Attending a post-secondary institution is a privilege. You have to work to earn the grades to get in, and you need to work to earn the money to pay for it. You can do this, and you'll be stronger for it.

Temptation (not the island)

Some days it seems like everyone else on campus is driving RAV4s, wearing Gore-Tex jackets and leather boots, and drinking $5 lattes. Do you really think all of them are rich, or have no debt? In my experience, the students who spend the most can afford it the least. These students, while appearing carefree and wealthy, are very likely to have high student debt. They are more concerned with looking good and living the high life than being financially secure. When I heard other students in class talking about how they were jetting down to California for the weekend to relax I turned green with envy – until they mentioned they were paying for it when their student loans came in!

Most students could afford their education without loans simply by cutting down on their expenses. Obviously there are cases where students are so destitute going into university that they are way behind the eight ball before they even start. Others have disabilities that may prevent them from working too many hours, and still others are single parents who have unavoidable expenses such as childcare. If this applies to you, graduating debt-free might not be realistic, but the information in this book will still help you take control of your situation.

For the majority of students, resisting the temptation to be like everyone else – to party at expensive bars, wear designer clothes, and eat at trendy restaurants – is going to be key in their struggle to find financial freedom while attaining the education they want to build a career. There is plenty of time to party after graduation when you have a steady income and no tuition to pay!

Try not to compare yourself with others too much. There will always be someone wealthier, smarter, or more talented than you are. It's a fact of life. If you constantly compare yourself to those with more, you'll never be satisfied with what you have and what you've accomplished. The flip side is also true. Compare yourself with those who have less than you and you may be content not to strive for more. For instance, sometimes we would make purchasing decisions that would cost us dearly, but because we were doing better than many of our friends, we justified the expense because "we're still not as broke as they are." Set your own goals based on what you want out of life and decide what role money will play. Don't let anyone else make those decisions for you.

Spending money to save money

Throughout the rest of this book, I want you to shift your focus. Keith used to accuse me of spending money to save money. I'd find a great sale, and buy a $50 item for just $25. I thought I saved $25. I didn't – I spent $25. Saving $25 would have been putting that money in a bank

Adbusters

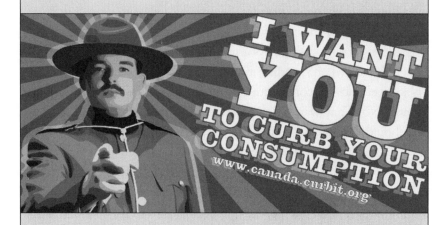

Adbusters describes itself as "a global network of artists, activists, writers, pranksters, students, educators, and entrepreneurs who want to advance the new social activist movement of the information age." Their lofty aim is to "topple existing power structures and forge a major shift in the way we will live in the 21st century." A non-profit organization, they publish a magazine, run a Web site, and create advertising campaigns designed to get across their message.

Adbusters is also behind Buy Nothing Day, held on the first day after the American Thanksgiving, the unofficial opening of the Christmas shopping season. To bring attention to our increasingly out of control holiday spending, participants refrain from buying anything for twenty-four hours. Each year, more and more people get involved, and more media attention is given to the campaign. However, most major U.S. television stations refuse to sell them ad space for it, proving once again just how much influence big-money advertisers have over our media.

A desire to educate people about the effects of our over-consumption and obsession with material wealth is at the heart of the Adbusters fight. For information or to get involved, visit www.adbusters.org.

account. Even though I'm aware of this sales technique, I still fall for it. I frequently find myself gravitating towards a sale rack of purses, even though I have ten already.

Our society thinks it's focused on saving money, with dollar stores, Wal-Mart stores, and Bay Days around every corner. But the truth is our society is focused on spending money. All the commercials, ads, and flyers we see – do the companies behind them really want us to save our money? No. They want us to spend it on their products. As a student you shouldn't focus on saving, but on spending. Instead of celebrating how much you saved, celebrate how little you spent. It's not just semantics; it's a strategy that can change your bankbook dramatically.

If the item you're buying is something you already intended to buy, you should be happy because you spent little, but don't ever compare it to what you could have spent. Instead of buying a $20 pair of jeans and being happy with them, you'll buy the $100 pair at half price and think you got a great deal – but you didn't, you lost $30.

Who thought these up anyway?

Shop now and save. If you're shopping, you're not saving.

On the twelfth day of giving… You might have heard the furor over this version of the Twelve Days of Christmas on a Canada Post commercial. Were they trying to be politically correct by removing the word Christmas, or were they commercializing the holidays even further than they already are?

Shopping is good. This major Canadian department store's slogan is representative of all things evil in today's society. Love is good, education is good, family is good, reading is good, but trust me, shopping is not good.

Live better, spend less. Again from a major department store. Yes you can live better and spend less, but it isn't going to happen shopping at a department store.

By attending a post-secondary institution you are investing in your future. You're announcing to the world that you want an education, you want to improve your chances of landing a great job, and you want to expand your horizons. You're taking steps to ensure a better future for yourself by looking ahead and planning for the long term. The same thing goes for working. When you work or volunteer during school, you're investing in your career. You're creating contacts and job prospects, building your resumé, and improving your employability.

In fact, a lot of the reasoning behind graduating with little debt is future-oriented. You want to graduate without debt so you can start your life with a rosy financial outlook. It's all about the future.

Or not. Sometimes, you've just got to focus on the now.

Whether you're in a two-year, four-year, or ten-year program, a lot of the things you do will follow the "Good Enough for Now" principle. Need to buy a winter jacket? Don't buy an expensive outfit that will last ten years. Buy a cheap one that will last you to the day you graduate. Buy something Good Enough for Now. Need a computer desk? The $20 one at the Salvation Army is Good Enough for Now. The same goes for clothes, cars, school supplies, furniture, etc. Anytime you need to purchase something, look for something inexpensive. You'll have plenty of time after you've graduated to buy better quality, higher prestige items if you want.

2 + 2 = 4. Watching Your Money!

The first practical tool I want focus on is what I call "Watching Your Money." How can you manage your money effectively if you don't know what you're doing with it? How many times have you taken cash out of a bank machine only to find your pockets empty hours later, and you can't remember what you bought? Watching Your Money, or WYM, is a budgeting strategy, though I hate the word. It makes me think of penny counting, Mr. Noodle, and hours with a calculator. I barely passed high school math, almost knocking myself out of the race for university because of poor calculus skills. A failing grade in a statistics course adds to my pathetic credentials as a mathematical guru.

And though I can't remember what seven times six is to save my soul, I can watch my money, and so can you.

Watching Your Money is incredibly easy, but I'll be honest, it's a bit of a pain. For it to work, everything you earn or spend must be recorded in the right category. It also has to be updated every day or two because if you let it get behind, it's very difficult to catch up. However, this is really a small investment of time for a big payback in savings. You'll figure out where you spend your money, where you're going to need to spend your money, and how you can trim expenses.

There are many different ways to set up a system, and no way is really the right way, as long as you are committed to managing it. You have to create a system that you'll use religiously, and something that is easy to understand. I tried saving all of my receipts in a book, but found it hard to divide everything into categories, anticipate what bills were coming due, or even figure out the total amount spent on things month by month. I also tried splitting money into envelopes for certain expenses, but then I just stole from the other envelopes when one ran short. Finally I began using Microsoft Excel, a simple spreadsheet program that came with my computer, and that worked great. If you don't have Excel or a similar worksheet program on your computer, you can download budgeting software for free off the Internet at www.download.com. If you don't have a computer, you can create a similar spreadsheet with graph paper and a pen, but you'll also need a basic calculator to add up the totals.

If you're very well organized, you can probably divide your tracking sheet into months. While in school I divided mine into weeks. This system gave me a good idea of what times of the month I needed cash the most, and when I could slide by with $5 in our account until payday.

These days I track my income and expenses monthly. I have two columns – one for the monthly plan, and one for reality. I can always see how much in one area I've already spent, and how much more I have to spend.

> **REALITY CHECK:** Use the worksheet below to figure out what's going to happen to your money for the year. Estimate your expenses as best as you can. If

you're not planning on working while in school, include your loan money under income. If you've got a car, add in the payments, insurance, gas, and maintenance costs. Fill in the very necessities of life, and see what's left over. The money not absolutely required for the necessities should be divided into two savings accounts, one for tuition, and one for books.

Totals	Actual	Budgeted
Income		1000
Expenses		905
Income less expenses		**95**

Income Source	Actual	Budgeted
Pay		1000
Line of credit		0
Total income		1000

Fixed Expenses	Actual	Budgeted
Rent		350
Utilities		85
Phone		30
Groceries		150
Tenant insurance		10
Bus pass		55
Bank service charges		5
Eating out		25
Gifts		25
Clothes		50
Household items		20
Entertainment		75
Health		25
Total expenses		**905**

You're now Watching Your Money. Do this for awhile. Beginning today, even if you're not in school yet, record everything you spend your money on – an easy task with credit card or debit purchases, a little harder with cash.

Watching Your Money is like exercising. It's difficult, it's not fun, but you know you should be doing it, and it does have its rewards.

You'll be surprised at what you're spending your money on. For instance, I was a big Coca-Cola drinker, and it remains one of my luxury items. Until I compiled all of my expenses into a tracking sheet, I had no idea how much money I was giving to the Coca-Cola Company every single month. I was shocked. Though I occasionally bought pop by the case, more often I bought single cans or bottles at convenience stores, movie theatres, and restaurants. A couple of bucks here and there didn't seem like a big deal, I mean, it was just pop, right? I was so naïve.

My two-to-three bottle a day habit was costing me an average of $3 a day, or $90 a month, or $1,080 a year. The equivalent of two university courses. So although I consider myself a die-hard Coca-Cola addict, I cut back on my daily fix. Instead of buying individual cans I bought two-litre bottles when they were on sale, and I made them last. A $90 a month expense dropped to $10 a month. Had I not forced myself to write down my expenses, I would have remained oblivious to this drain on my cash. By WYM, you'll find these cash-draining expenses, and throughout this book you'll find ways to cut or eliminate them.

There's another practical reason for Watching Your Money. Scholarship committees and the loan gods frequently request proof of financial need. They want you to demonstrate that you're not wasting the money you earned or the money they've given you. Creating a tracking sheet proves that you're not only organized, but also highly motivated and responsible. Beware of the temptation to fudge the truth (or flat out lie) in the sheet you submit for scrutiny. If you've really spent a lot of money in areas you think they will disapprove of, examine your spending habits. No one expects you to be an absolute social recluse, but just because that hot leather jacket was 50% off doesn't mean you should spend $350 on it.

After a few months of Watching Your Money, I hope you'll have found it a useful tool for understanding where your money goes. While it gets easier with practice, there are still times today when I know I've been on too much of a spending spree and I'm hesitant to check my banking statement and update my spreadsheet. But I refuse to let myself ignore my own financial flaws. Sure it hurts to have the expense for that $100 night out jump off the page at you when you're cleaning the couch for bus fare, but the truth hurts, and recognizing your mistakes will help you get schooled (pun intended, sorry).

Grab your library card

Don't Spend Your Raise by Dara Duguay is the best personal finance book I've ever read. The book offers sixty rules for dealing with money, regardless of your income or employment status. Each rule has an accompanying chapter, and it's written in a practical and down-to-earth way. *Don't Spend Your Raise* will change the way you shop, save, and think about money, and it's a must-read for anyone interested in taking control of their finances.

One more thing

Keep your eye on your goal – to graduate without going into debt. When temptation arises, be strong! Resist consumerism-driven urges to spend your money on unnecessary material goods. In the long run, your life will be richer for it. Your education is what you make of it, and I know you will succeed once you put your mind to it.

CHAPTER TWO
C-A-P-I-T-A-L-I-S-M

This chapter, while covering some "new student" content, shouldn't be skipped over if you're already in school. Here I'll cover some general thoughts for you to keep in mind when reading the rest of this book. You'll learn the best mindset to have as a student, and your first steps to take entering an educational institution.

Mindset, not mind meld

Most self-help books want you to fill out pages and pages of worksheets to determine the kind of person you are before you begin your journey toward whatever it is the book wants you to accomplish. I'm going to make it easy for you. Grab a pen, and agree or disagree with each of the following statements:

- I am a weak person, easily manipulated by the media and my peers.
- I am too immature to handle the responsibilities of acquiring an education.
- I am content to follow the crowd, even when I can't afford it and it threatens my future financial situation.

- I don't want to be accountable for my income or my spending. I'd rather pretend everything is okay even when it's not.

Okay, I'm not very good at this personal discovery thing. I expect you disagreed with all of these statements. Yet often we make decisions that, when stripped down to the bare bones, are guided by the kind of thinking above. For a short while I refused to balance my chequebook. I wasn't sure how much money we had, or whether we would have enough to cover the bills and my spending. I was agreeing with the last statement, and hiding from reality.

Trying to get your education while displaying any of the above behaviours is going to be impossibly difficult. You have to be proactive, responsible, and aware of your situation, even when you'd rather stick your head in the sand.

Though tuition is rising, graduating with minimal debt is still possible for most students. Each and every choice you make counts, from where you go to school to where you buy your sneakers. Each decision you make matters. If you have wealthy friends who like to party and try to pressure you into blowing your money at the bars with them, remind yourself that you have made a personal decision to value different priorities. They won't be around to bail you out when you can't make your monthly payments after graduation. Your decision about how to spend your entertainment money, and how much you spend, is just that – it's your decision, not anyone else's.

You are not what you wear. And you are not what your parents have bought you. Try not to measure your success in terms of material things. Measure it by your accomplishments, your achievement of your goals, your kindness, your intelligence, your talents, or your ability to help others.

One of those successes is going to be completing your post-secondary education. And while I can provide you with many tips and tricks, resources, and tools to increase your income, decrease your spending, and navigate through your educational career, you are the one who has to make the tough calls.

Expert advice on money

John Caspar is a Vice President and Investment Advisor with CIBC Wood Gundy. He is also the money analyst for the *CTV News at Five* in Vancouver, and he pens an award-winning personal finance column, *The Smart Money*. John has been a featured financial expert on BCTV, CBC Newsworld, and Global TV, as well as various print and radio media. John has also served on the Board of Directors for the Canadian Association of Financial Planners and has been an instructor and course development advisor for the Canadian Securities Institute. I think you get the picture – he knows his stuff, and here's his advice.

"You want to pay down your debt and save money, but you can't. You've got bills a-go-go, the world keeps getting more expensive, and Mr. Slate down at the quarry won't give you a raise. So what do you do? The good news is that there's very likely something you can do. The bad news is that you won't like it. And I know this, by the way, because I don't like it. Are you ready? Here comes the thing you can do: spend less. See? We hate that." John identifies five steps to saving money, or spending less, and they apply to students just as much as anyone else.

John's five steps

Don't think about what's hard or easy – think about what's right. And once you've made up your mind about what you're going to do, don't tell yourself for even one second that you're going to try. Just go do it.

1. **Evaluate your needs.**
    Not your wants. Not your conveniences. Not your luxuries. Just your needs. Don't make value judgements here. Never mind what's nice, what you prefer, what you're used to, what you could never get used to, what you expect. Needs. You should find this to be a very short list. Once you're finished, go through it again and challenge yourself to strip it down further.

2. **Evaluate your income.**

    How much do you make from all sources?

3. **Evaluate your expenses.**

    There are two approaches to this. You can either calculate your actual expenses, or you can track your actual expenditures. If you think you have a serious spending problem (as in, "I don't know where the money goes!"), the second approach is a good idea. Make a deal with yourself and whoever else lives in your household that you'll get a written receipt or make a note for every single nickel you spend for a month. At the end of thirty days, you'll know what you spent and where. And you may be surprised at how your expenses and your needs are incompatible.

4. **Start cutting.**

    This is the hard part for most people. It is, in fact, why only a small percentage of people are successful. You have lots of Joneses in your life to keep up with. The messages from advertisers and the lifestyles of your neighbours and co-workers may create strong desires to share in the "fun" and consumption. It's a powerful attraction. That's why it's vital to have clearly decided in writing what you really want to save. You need the tools of clarity and precision to fight the temptation to misspend. Cut, slash, and burn. Everything must go if there's no dough.

5. **Repeat.**

    This is the final step, and the most important. Any good plan needs revisiting again and again. Is the strategy still working? Are you slipping anywhere? Has something important changed? Can you combine strategies to speed up your progress, i.e. cut back and make more? Be creative! You need to do this anyway, so you might as well have fun with it.

It seems glib to suggest that there is only one road to financial success. But the essential principles are often conceptually very simple. They're just hard to implement and live by.

Choosing the right post-secondary program

Oddly enough, tuition isn't going to be your main concern when choosing a program. Tuition varies widely at schools across Canada. Simon Fraser University's tuition for a general arts program, including fees, is $3,091 a year, while at Acadia, the same program is $6,905 including fees. But tuition isn't the primary issue. It's living expenses, the time commitment to your program, and employment opportunities in your city. A one-year program with a $20,000 price tag might be a better buy than a four-year program that costs the same. You'll definitely have to get a loan to pay the $20,000 up front, but you'll get into the workforce faster, and could even pay the loan off before you would have graduated from the four-year program.

"A university education is superior to a college education." Pompous university students are generally the people who propagate this myth. But universities, colleges, and technical schools offer different programs, and are hardly comparable these days. For instance, if you want to be an electrician, why waste time learning philosophy at a university? Go to a technical school, where you learn in a hands-on environment in less time and for less money. However, if you want to be a university professor, you've got to go to university. What kind of learner are you? Do you learn from books, professors, or practical experience? Different people are better suited to different learning environments. Don't let anyone tell you that your choice is inferior to another. I always wondered if a two-year journalism program would have been a better educational program for me, and to this day I wonder if I should go back to school.

Have you decided what you want to major in? Talk to people in your prospective field and ask them which program they would recommend. Contact potential employers and find out what their requirements are. You can also browse through newspaper classifieds, looking for interesting positions and making note of their educational requirements. Web sites like www.monster.ca list jobs of all disciplines, and are another good source for your research. The Government of Canada has created a great Web site for students at www.canlearn.ca. Here you'll find information on how to plan and pay for your education, as well as other valuable resources for students. You'll also find the Student Planner, an interactive tool that will walk you through the process of choosing the right program and the right school, based on your interests. You may have already done something like this in high school, but if it's been awhile, or you've never completed one, it might be useful to help you narrow down a field of interest.

Remember that any type of education is a bad investment if it turns out you have the wrong degree for the career you desire. In addition, many colleges and technical schools are combining their programs with universities, blurring the distinctions between diploma and degree, and between two-year and four-year programs.

From a financial standpoint, a shorter program is a wise decision. You can get a full-time job after graduation and save up until you can afford to go to university if you still want a degree. Many two-year programs easily transfer to a university program, giving you credit for your completed work. If you're the type of person who bores easily or changes his mind often, locking yourself into a four- or five-year program could frustrate you and result in your dropping out. In the end, the decision has to be yours. Although it used to be true that a university degree resulted in higher corporate recognition, it's not always the case anymore. Don't let anyone, including well-meaning friends and family, pressure you into an educational path you're not committed to, simply because of old-school notions of status.

> **REALITY CHECK:** Approximately 70% of students at any given school were living in the area before they began attending. If you have the option to live at home, it will be extremely difficult to attend a school out of town without getting loans. You'll have all the extra costs associated with not living at home, plus you may pay higher tuition because you are from another province. You'll have higher phone bills, moving costs, and additional travel expenses. Unfortunately, most university and college planning books don't deal with this issue, encouraging you to consider any university, regardless of location. You need to consider location. If

your parents have offered to let you live at home while going to school, go to a school where you can use this resource. If you're moving out of the house for school, consider other factors. If part-time office clerk jobs in Halifax are hard to come by and pay $5.50 an hour, while the same jobs in Edmonton are plentiful and pay $12.00 an hour, go west young man.

If you plan on being a doctor, maybe you think it's vital to attend the top medical school in Canada instead of your local school. During my time at the University of Calgary, I met many students who moved to Calgary to take programs there instead of schools closer to home – and they were in general programs! While *Maclean's* magazine may gain kudos and recognition for their annual ranking of Canadian universities, don't place too much importance on the status of your school. Going away for school could actually be detrimental. What if you end up dropping out because you miss living in your hometown with your friends and family? If you don't live in your school city for the whole program but move back home to work after graduation, you won't have made any networking connections, or built up local job experience. Who will employers be more impressed with – the candidate who attended a prestigious school but was so academically

---

University Planning for Canadians for Dummies

One of the most comprehensive books I've ever found on the topic of higher education is *University Planning for Dummies for Canadians*. Complete with the familiar screaming yellow cover, this book is a great reference tool for high school students and their parents. It covers everything from researching degrees, schools, and even teachers, to filling out application forms, scholarship forms, and loan forms. While some of the information is 100% contrary to my ideas (like not factoring in living expenses when considering a school), it is a must-read if you haven't figured out all the details yet about which school you want to attend.

focused that he has no practical experience, or the student who went to an average school and spent his more abundant free time volunteering and working in the industry?

Not your only option – alternative schooling

If you're in a four-year program, you don't necessarily have to graduate in four years. I took an extra year to finish, and Keith took three! In Keith's case, while one year was the result of a faculty change, the other two years were planned. He had a good job and wanted to work enough to pay for school. By not taking a full load of classes, he managed to work more hours, and owe less for tuition and books. If the option is available, taking extra time to graduate is a great way to ease your reliance on government money. Most employers won't even blink, and if they do comment on it, tell them the truth. Your priority was to graduate with a manageable debt load and this was the best option, or you wanted to focus on improving your experience in your field and needed the extra time to balance the two.

Here's something else to think about. How fast do you want to enter the "real world"? I was twenty-three when I started the job I'm in now. I was the youngest person in the department, even in a company with a very young workforce. And while it hasn't been too big a problem lately, my age often worked against me in many other jobs. As a young person, you can run the risk of not being taken seriously because it's hard for others to believe you have the experience and wisdom to make important contributions. If you stay on campus an extra year, you'll be another year older, another year wiser, and hopefully a little less broke.

What about taking a year off between high school and post-secondary? Like applying for a credit card to build a credit history, taking a year off to save money for school can be very dangerous. You may just find yourself unintentionally abusing the opportunity. If you are very committed to your education and think this is the only way to build the bankroll you need for school, it's definitely an option. Most schools won't penalize you, but check first. You don't want to lose your spot in an in-demand faculty.

The danger of taking time off from your studies is obvious – you might never go back. Once you start making a full-time salary, you may never want to return to the starving student lifestyle. Your savings likely won't grow as quickly as you hoped if you're suddenly distanced from school and it doesn't seem so urgent anymore. You may also lose the knowledge needed for further classes. It's amazing how rapidly theory disappears from your memory once you're in the real world.

Have you considered correspondence? The University of Athabasca is an accredited university in Alberta that offers courses through mail or online. One of their courses could be taken as credit for my faculty, so I thought I'd try it. Not only was the course $50 less, but books were included in the fee, saving me another $75. The course was easier than I expected, and instead of spending thirty-plus hours in a classroom, I had just about the same amount of reading required as in any other course, but without the class time (or at least the guilt about missing class time). I finished the course quickly, got the credit, and saved myself a ton of valuable time.

Your parents had it better than you

Since your parents went to college, tuition has increased as much as tenfold, but that hasn't discouraged young Canadians from pursuing higher education. One in twenty Canadians, or approximately 1.7 million people, are post-secondary students. Average student debt among those students who borrow and graduate from four-year programs is approximately $21,000.

> **REALITY CHECK:** Tuition levels don't affect university enrolment. Nova Scotia universities have the highest tuition and highest participation rates. British Columbia has very low tuition, and very low participation rates.

If your parents went to college or university, they probably relied on parental support to pay for their schooling. They likely didn't work and didn't take out sizeable loans. You probably won't have it so easy.

Statistics show that almost all students work during the summer and nearly half also work during the school year. But over the past ten years, the percentage of students working and the number of hours they work haven't really changed, though their reliance on student loans and other types of credit has.

The real survivor

If you're lucky, your parents will be able to help you with your expenses during school. But even if mom and dad don't give you a cheque every September, you'll still need their support and that of others around you. It would have been a lot harder for me going though school without a network of friends and family. Their help is invaluable.

Relying on friends and family for help can be a humbling experience. Here you are, trying to be mature, responsible, and self-sufficient, while hanging your underwear to dry in your parent's basement. Sometimes it'll be something small you need, like a ride, laundry detergent, a sweater. Other times your request will be bigger: money, a loaner car, or a load of groceries.

Most people won't think twice about lending or giving you something you need to help you get through school without going into debt. They want to see you succeed, and if they have the resources, they'll be happy to help.

Graciously accepting offers of help is a skill you should learn early. Let people help you. They want to, and you need the help. There is a fine line, though, between accepting genuine offers of assistance and being a freeloader. Know the line and don't cross it, or watch offers of assistance dwindle to zero.

Have you ever tried to treat a friend to dinner and had her fight with you over the bill? It's her birthday, you made the invite, and she's trying to pay. It can feel better to give than to receive, and it's frustrating to the person who wants to give when the receiver isn't gracious.

One of the pitfalls of leaning on friends is the tendency to do it when you don't really need to. You definitely don't want a reputation as someone who always bums off others rather than doing things yourself. If you're asking for money, a service, or a favour because you can't afford it, make sure you really can't. How would you feel if you gave a friend $100 to cover his shortfall in rent money, and found out he went out bar-hopping two nights later? If you tell your family you can't afford to exchange gifts but show up for Christmas dinner with a new jacket, they won't have much sympathy for you. Make sure you have your priorities in order. Show respect to those you're asking favours of, and they'll feel like their gifts were wisely given.

Thank them twice

When you lean on friends for big things, like carpooling, cash, etc., you have a responsibility to thank them – twice. The first time you thank them is immediately after the favour or loan. The first thank you is verbal: when you have their attention, say thank you and be sincere.

The second thank you is more difficult. Now you've got to show them your appreciation and pay back the favour. You may not be in the position to thank them appropriately right away; you might not be able to thank them until you've had a full-time job for a few months and started to gain ground financially. But as soon as you can, make sure you let the people who helped you know how much you appreciated their assistance. There's no scorecard. If your parents gave you $1,000 for tuition, you don't need to pay them back or spend $1,000 on a gift for them. But your second thank you is a form of paying them back. Give them a gift certificate, take your younger siblings out for a day to give them time alone, treat them to dinner, or make sure you're available when they need you.

Depressed yet? Why your education is worth it

Post-secondary graduates have higher incomes and lower rates of unemployment than non-graduates. On average, university graduates earn considerably more than other post-secondary institution graduates; however, college graduates usually make quicker transitions to the workforce than university graduates. Think getting a Management degree will ensure you make loads more money than an English graduate? Wrong. While the Management grad may make a higher salary initially, recent studies have shown that the salary gap tends to narrow after ten to fifteen years in the workforce.

Make the most of your educational career. You're paying for an education, so make sure you get one. Skipping a class to pick up an extra shift to pay for the class is one thing. Skipping a class to hit the pub is another. When choosing options, select courses you're interested in, or that will challenge you to learn something new. Ask questions in class and make an effort to get to know your professors. You'll learn more about the subject, have an ally when you need assistance on an assignment, and create a contact for later reference needs. And don't waste your time. If you don't know what you want to do with your life, spending money on classes you dislike or flunk isn't the most effective way to find out.

Money trap: student credit cards

Almost 67% of Canadian post-secondary students possess at least one credit card and almost 40% report carrying debt on those cards. It's easy to get a credit card. The credit card companies set up booths around campus for the first month of classes offering free gift certificates, clothing, and other incentives just for applying. The interest rates are high – 17% or more is standard. A first-year student with no credit and no job will usually get approved for a card, even without a co-signer.

The banks set the initial limit on the card fairly low, but if you make the minimum monthly payments, they'll increase your credit limit without even checking to see if you want it increased. I never paid much attention to the limit on my first credit card until I wanted to buy a stereo and thought it might be over the limit. I checked a statement and discovered my limit had been steadily increasing and was at $5,000! At the time, that was six month's salary, and way too much temptation. I called the bank and had it dropped back down to $500. Sometimes the best way to avoid temptation is to get rid of it altogether.

Expert Advice — Gary Foreman

Gary Foreman is the editor of *Dollar Stretcher*, a newsletter with an online presence at www.dollarstretcher.com. A former Certified Financial Planner, Gary has a lot of advice for students thinking about getting a credit card to build up their credit rating. Some of his advice includes:

Consider why you need to build credit. Typically, the only time that you really need good credit is when you want to borrow money. In fact, you probably won't need to have much of a credit history until you want to finance a major purchase like furniture, an auto, or home. So there's probably no hurry to build credit.

Having a credit card does not necessarily help your credit rating. If you get a card with a low credit limit and pay your bill in full each month, you will begin to improve your credit score. But that same credit card could also hurt your credit score. All you have to do is begin to carry a monthly balance. In fact, if you just have a credit limit that's too high in relation to your income, you will be less attractive to future potential lenders.

A credit card is a dangerous tool. Less than 50% of all credit card accounts held by students are paid off each month. It's very easy to charge a few things during the month only to find that you don't have enough money to pay the bill when it comes. If you feel you can't use credit responsibly, you would be wise to wait.

When you do get a card, leave it at home. The only time you need it is when you have planned to make a specific purchase and you know that you have the money to pay for it. Carrying the card with you is an invitation to make impulse purchases.

Move cautiously. Most students are not building credit – they're damaging their credit worthiness and digging a financial hole that will make it hard to rent apartments and buy cars when they graduate.

Plan ahead (though it's probably too late)

If you bought or received this book before starting your post-secondary education, you're ahead of the game. You've got two things to do:

Get a job. Working while you're in high school is important for two reasons. First, it gives you something to put on your university and scholarship applications. It shows character, drive, and ability. Second, it provides you with a paycheque.

Start saving now. University costs money, and you won't be making much while you're in school. The more you have saved before you start, the easier it will be to get through school without debt. Whether you're in grade nine or twelve, don't put off saving money for higher education. Put away a quarter, or half, of every paycheque, and don't touch that money. For motivation (and cash), ask your parents if they'll match that money. Or invest in a Registered Education Savings Plan (RESP). For every $2,000 you invest in an RESP, the government will throw in $400. The money invested isn't taxed until it's withdrawn. As you'll be withdrawing it when you're a low-income student, you probably still won't have to pay tax.

For tuition alone you'll need $5,000 to $6,000 a year, and if you're not living at home, your living expenses will be between $11,000 and $12,000. That's close to $20,000 a year, or $80,000 for a four-year program. Some people claim that not only does your education cost you tuition, fees, and living expenses, it also costs lost wages (because you can't work full-time). We could argue numbers all day, but the fact remains that the bills have to be paid. While I will stress over and over again the importance of earning an income while in school, you may still face a shortfall. Wouldn't it be nice if you had a savings account to fall back on?

But if you do save some money for school, don't just live off that money until you run out and then get a job. Keep your savings until you absolutely need the money. It will last longer, and you won't end up regretting having partied through your savings.

Parental assistance

If you haven't already talked to your parents about your future, do so. Do they want to, or can they, help you pay for your education? Have they saved any money, or can they give you assistance as you go through your program? If you choose a local school, will they let you live at home, and will you have to pay rent? When applying for both scholarships and government assistance you'll need to show proof of

---

Six Days to a New Couch

Have you ever played Six Degrees of Kevin Bacon? I have, and I suck at it. The theory is that everyone is separated by less than six degrees or connections. Somehow, Kevin Bacon got thrown in as the connector. In my world, it's Six Days to a New Couch.

My theory is, if you want a new couch, the easiest way to get it is to ask around. Ask your hairdresser, your friends, your co-workers. Tell them what you're looking for and your price range. Odds are, they know someone who knows someone who has a couch you can have for free or for cheap. Every time I've ever needed something I was willing to take used, whether a couch, a fridge, or a bike, it's taken less than six days of asking around to find the thing I needed.

So you're not looking for a couch. That's okay, Six Days to a New Couch will work for pretty much anything. A couch, a job, or an apartment – asking around gets things done fast and cheap. When a girlfriend lost her basement suite renter, she called to see if I knew anyone looking for a place. I did. My brother was looking, and he moved in two weeks later. Instead of spending money on placing ads and interviewing strangers, she saved her money and even found someone she already knew and trusted.

The same thing goes if you have something for sale. When we bought our dining room chairs, a glass-topped table came with them for free. Looking to get rid of it, we asked around to see if anyone wanted to buy a table. Unfortunately we asked too many people, and now four friends are fighting over who gets it!

---

parental financial assistance or provide reasons why it isn't there, so you might as well find out now what you're up against.

If your parents can afford it, they have a responsibility to provide assistance. Their responsibility isn't a moral one, it's actually government mandated. Here's a thought: if your parents can pay your whole way through school, should they? We all had friends whose parents gave them everything – a new car on their sixteenth birthday, clothes, credit cards, and other valuable things. Usually, the things were lost, broken, or driven into a light pole. When you're given something, you just don't give it the respect and care you would have if you worked your butt off and bought it yourself. What does it matter to you if you fail a class if your parents are footing the bill?

Your parents may not be able to cover your tuition, but can they help in other ways? Can you live at home while going to school? Can you do your laundry at their place, borrow their car, and grocery shop in their pantry? Don't underestimate the value of these and other contributions. Having a family that supports you and wants you to live at home while in school is something many students would give anything to have.

When it's over

You get through school and you land a high-paying job. Isn't that the way it's supposed to work? Unfortunately, it's not that easy. Having a post-secondary education doesn't guarantee you a well-paying job. After graduation you have no guarantees you'll find a job that pays you enough to live on your own, drive a nice car, buy a big television, contribute to an RRSP, or achieve any of your financial or life goals.

Take Barbara for example. At thirty, she's a graduate of York University with a degree in English. During school she worked part-time jobs, and in the summers worked full-time. The money she made working, as well as support from her parents, enabled her to graduate without student loans. However, after graduation she found it "extremely disheartening when the only job I could land was cleaning toilets at the YMCA in Halifax for $5.50 an hour.

"After a few months of depression and frequent use of credit cards (that I conveniently received first year of university), I decided it was time to relocate and strive for a different occupation. I just couldn't understand why it was so difficult to find a decent job even with a university degree. I ended up in Banff, Alberta jumping from job to job as a maid when finally I made the decision to go back to school. I had to keep a tight budget since I needed first and last month's rent, utilities, food, and any other miscellaneous spending. Not to mention the minimum payment toward my credit card!

"The smartest thing I did was choosing to have a part-time job and work as much as possible. The more money I made during school the less I would have to pay back later. Working also kept me focused on my studies. It's a constant reminder to keep organized and complete projects on time, much like a professional career. I saved money on transportation and got some exercise by renting a room within walking distance of school. Using public transit also saved money rather than leasing a car, paying for insurance, and gas.

"The worst thing I did was use my credit card for some of the tuition. I also charged a used car on my credit card to move to my new job across the country, but at least I'm still driving it! It's a good thing I've continued to be frugal after graduation because after a year at my first job I was laid off. I've since been relying on employment insurance until I find another job that will start the next chapter of my many careers."

The moral of this story? Don't get in over your head with anything, whether it's spending, credit cards, loans, or even the pursuit of further education. Each decision you make will have an element of the unknown as a factor. If I get a loan, will I be able to pay it off? If I take a year off to work, will I still want to go back? Above all, don't make unrealistic assumptions about your salary post-graduation. If you're spending freely because you think paying it off will be easy once you have a well-paying full-time job, you'll be in serious trouble when that job doesn't materialize but the collection company does.

Clock Watching

You can call it time management, or day planning, but I call it Clock Watching. Clock Watching isn't about accounting for every minute of your life, but keeping you on top of things. You'll feel much less guilty about spending four hours in front of the TV if you know your week is under control deadline-wise. Due dates won't come as a surprise, you won't double-book an evening, and you may be able to schedule extra shifts at work when you find the time.

Clock Watching is also a strategic tool. Balancing work and school can be tricky, but if you plan your work and school strategically, you can usually fit both in with a little creativity.

For instance, some semesters I'd try to schedule all my classes on the Monday, Wednesday, and Friday block. You may be able to schedule Tuesday, Thursday, and Saturday. Or every morning with all afternoons off, or vice versa. Whatever you choose, you'll need to plan your class schedule carefully, and be strategic about it. You may have a job and need to plan your classes around that. If you're bartending nights, don't schedule any 8:00 a.m. classes. If you want to find an office job, choose evening and weekend classes, and group them to allow the maximum free business hours possible.

If almost every class fits perfectly in your schedule but the last one is full, don't give up. Take your schedule to the prof and let him know your situation. I've never had a prof turn down my request for entry into a class when it obviously gave me the schedule I needed to hold a job. A few people are going to drop out of the class anyway; you might as well get the spot early.

One more thing

If you're still reading this, you've proved a few things.

- You're a strong person, eagerly looking forward to the challenges of obtaining a post-secondary education.
- You understand the value of the educational program you're

considering or are enrolled in.

- You are confident in your ability to find creative ways to pay for that education.
- You will succeed!

CHAPTER THREE
Scholarships: Why You Deserve Them, Why You Won't Get Them

By far the easiest way to cover your biggest education cost, namely your tuition, is to get someone else do it. Ideally, someone who doesn't need the money back. This can be accomplished one of two ways. The first way is for your parents (or another wealthy relative) to foot the bill. The second way is to win scholarships.

Not all scholarships are created equal. Scholarships are cash awards distributed based on academic standing, financial need, extracurricular activity, or a combination of these three criteria. A prize is an award given in recognition of an accomplishment, and may be a book, plaque, or small cash amount. A bursary is similar to

---

$10 million in unclaimed scholarships!

Have you ever heard the claim that millions of dollars of scholarships go unused each year? Finaid.org dispels the myth. It stems from a study in 1997 by the National Institute of Work and Learning. The study estimated that a total of $7 billion was potentially available from employer tuition assistance programs, but that only about $300 million to $400 million was being used. This money isn't scholarship money open to any students. It's employer sponsored educational funding, and not really a scholarship at all by normal standards.

a scholarship, and is an award given based on academic merit and significant financial need.

Work = lower grades, lower grades = fewer scholarships

During the last year of high school I applied for a variety of entrance scholarships. The paperwork was sent with the university acceptance package, so it was easy to complete. I received a scholarship from the Alberta government, the Alexander Rutherford Scholarship, for less than $1,000. Most students I knew entering university were given a Rutherford Scholarship because if you were accepted into university, you likely had the grades required for it. I also applied for a few other scholarships, receiving just one. After my first year of university I applied for scholarships for the second year. I read books about scholarships for tips and guidance, and filled out more than a dozen applications, including the general application from the university. Unfortunately, I didn't receive any that second year.

In talking with other students, whenever the topic came up, I discovered a trend. Those students who did receive scholarships often were the ones who didn't work. Some had stellar grades because they didn't hold jobs during the school year and focused on their studies instead. Others played competitive sports instead of working and received athletic-based scholarships. And the final group? The people involved in community volunteer activities, again, not working for money.

Not being an athlete, I had two choices to secure scholarships. I could devote myself to school alone, or school and volunteering. For me, working part-time was out of the question if I wanted to keep my grades high enough for consideration.

I chose not to worry about scholarships. I reasoned that the only sure thing was work. I figured I could study my butt off, and still have a teacher hate me and reflect it in their grading. I didn't like the idea of putting my financial life in the hands of my profs. I also disliked the idea of devoting myself entirely to my studies. I believed experience would be valued over grades when it came time to find a real job. So I relied on employment to fund my education, and Keith did the same. A paycheque was a sure thing.

That's not to say I didn't keep applying for scholarships. I did, but work experience was never as highly valued as volunteer experience, and I didn't make the cut. Another student gave me a tip and told me that by joining a professional communication group as a student member, I would be considered for their scholarships. The $50 membership fee was covered by the $500 scholarship I won. And there ended the scholarship free ride, at least for me. All told, I probably spent just a weekend or two researching and writing to apply for these scholarships, and they covered

---

When profs go bad

Every student knows that if a prof has it out for you, you'll never make an A. Parents and non-students reading this might cry foul, but it happens. I once had a low-rate instructor give me a D, claiming I plagiarized an essay. When I approached her she refused to discuss it with me until I took the paper, and her written comments, to the Student Advisor office at the Student Union. University rules state that any student thought to be plagiarizing must be reported to the faculty and be given a failing grade. Technically a D wasn't a failing grade, and she hadn't reported me. Once I produced the notes and proved I could expound further on the theories outlined in the paper, she was to have it graded by another professor. The grade improved, but that didn't help my other marks in the class, which were suspiciously lower than any other class I was in. It put a substandard grade on my transcript, and there wasn't anything I could do about it. What if I had been relying on that class to maintain a perfect grade point average?

Profs are human – they can lower your marks if they don't agree with your position or don't like you personally. The flip side is also true. In my experience, getting an A with a certain prof guaranteed I'd get an A in the next class with him, despite not trying nearly as hard. For some profs, once they get it in their books that you're an A student, you'll always be one.

---

the cost of a few classes. If you've got what it takes to get scholarships – good grades, community involvement, talent, or other highly developed skills – you should definitely take a few days each semester to apply. A little investment in time could pay off big in cold hard cash.

How to get free money

Most scholarship books and Web sites will request that you mail in a request for information, and they'll send you an application package to complete. Since scholarships are given out all year, you can keep an eye on the deadlines and apply as they become available. If you find one that's perfect but you've missed the deadline, add the information to your file. Rarely do scholarship committees accept late applications. If you've missed the deadline, try again next year.

Does not meet criteria

During high school I noticed a scholarship given by the *Calgary Herald* to students who had worked newspaper routes. Though I hadn't delivered the paper, I had written for it. As one of the *Herald*'s freelance/part-time/unpaid youth writers, I thought I'd apply anyway, explaining in my essay why I was applying though I technically didn't meet the criteria. Wouldn't you know it, I received the scholarship. The $300 wasn't a lot of money, but it did pay for my books during my first semester of school.

Who can help

When I want to learn about something, the first place I go is the bookstore. But not to buy books. I rarely purchase new books, only buying titles I know I can't find in a used bookstore, or I know I'll use as a reference. Instead I scan the shelves, look for the most interesting books, and write down the titles and authors. Then I hit the library to reserve those same books.

I like researching a topic by reading books because I can do it on my own time, and find out the answers to questions I'm sure are dumb. Once I've read everything I can on a topic, I'll start surfing the Internet to find additional information. While I don't know how we survived without the Internet for research, it's still a black hole, sucking in good intentions and valuable time. Instead of researching scholarships, I ended up playing Lemonade Stand for hours.

Online research. If you have more willpower than I do, search the Internet first. Whatever you find can be copied and pasted into a Word document, saving you time copying everything out by hand from a library book. For one-stop shopping, your best bet is www.studentawards.com. A free service designed to help you find every scholarship under the sun, it also lists contests for tuition money. Simply visit the site and create a personal profile. The system will find scholarships applicable to you, and even draft personalized letters to the scholarship committee requesting an application package. It will also send you e-mail notices when new scholarships matching your profile are entered into the system. Another Web site, www.scholarshipscanada.com, also offers a free scholarship search, with a more complex registration form. At www.myschool101.com you can create a custom search or search quickly by keyword, with no registration required. Scholarship hunting doesn't get much easier.

Libraries and bookstores. Your school or city library will have a few books on scholarships, but they may be out of date or reserved when you need them. Your next stop is the school bookstore. They always have a section on scholarships, writing essays, and taking your SATs. Grab the newest and most comprehensive book, find a corner where you can sit and read, and flip through the book looking for scholarships you're eligible for. Many of them you'll probably have already found online, but if you find any that aren't, record the information so you can apply later.

On-campus help. Another good resource is your school financial aid office, which can provide you with help finding scholarships, completing the applications, and even reviewing your final submission. Just don't visit the week before tuition is due, or the week before the scholarship application deadline. They'll be too busy processing student loans and scholarship applications to have time for a one-on-one with you.

Your school financial aid office is also where you can pick up a comprehensive scholarship application form, if your school has one. This form allows you to fill out one application, but be considered for a variety of scholarships. You may still be required to write an essay or two, so pick this form up early and complete it right away. Your school calendar will probably have the due date for this application included in it. At the U of C, scholarships were also posted on a bulletin board outside the financial services office, and often they were scholarships not listed in any other places. Copy the info, but play fair – don't steal the poster!

Word of mouth. The final way to find scholarships is – say it with me now – to ask around. Your employer, or your parents' employers, might offer a scholarship to employees or children of employees. If your parents belong to a professional or sports organization, you may qualify for a scholarship. There are a lot of scholarships out there for students who meet very specific criteria, and there are just as many general scholarships.

Brett is a graduate of the University of Calgary's Geology program. While attending school, he landed a great scholarship because of his dad. "My dad is a firefighter, and a scholarship is offered to children of firefighters. I had to keep my grades up, but the scholarship was $2,500 a year. I decided to live at home while going to school, and my expenses were minimal. The scholarship covered most of my expenses during the school year, and I made enough money each summer to cover tuition, books, and the rest of my living expenses. I didn't have to work part-time during the year and instead devoted myself to getting good grades. I graduated without owing any money to student loans, and within a year I had bought a great house with a 20% down payment. Instead of living the party life during school and being stuck paying back loans for years, I put that money into my house, and now I have the time, the money, and the energy to really enjoy myself."

Apply yourself

You've got the scholarship application – now what? Follow these general tips to create a deserving application.

- Provide everything required. Your application might be tossed because you forgot to provide your Social Insurance Number.

Surly public servant

What is it about being a public servant that can turn nice people into sour bureaucrats the minute they start their workday? While most university employees are wonderful, helpful people, you'll also run into some surly, impatient jerks. I used to be meek, and I would apologize for bothering them with questions and slink away. Then one day I had an epiphany – in the middle of the fees line-up.

The woman rolling her eyes at my questions worked for me. As a university employee, with her salary being paid by the university and the government, I was paying her salary through my tuition and taxes. In essence, I was her boss.

While my first instinct was to say something insulting and insolent, I asked to speak to the supervisor, and calmly explained my frustration at being treated rudely. ("I'm so sorry to bother you, but I was speaking with Ms. X and she seemed annoyed with my questions. I'm not finding out what I need to know, is there someone else here who could help me?")

The key to having people respond to you is being overly friendly rather than overly psychotic. So the next time you run into a nasty school employee, don't be afraid to ask for assistance from someone else, and let the supervisor or manager know that this person's behaviour is unacceptable. They're working for you after all.

- Look the part. Write neatly, or type everything with a Times New Roman 12-point font on decent quality white paper. You're not in kindergarten so leave the pink stationery and stickers in the desk drawer.
- Complete the application on time, and mail it in well before the deadline.
- Keep a copy of your application for future use, backup, or reference.
- Make it personal. Target your essay, resumé, or letter to the award criteria.
- Accentuate, promote, and highlight your qualifications, but never lie or exaggerate too much.
- Proofread it twice.

Submitting the application

It shouldn't take you more than a few days to research and request more information on scholarships you meet the criteria for. When you receive an application package, complete it right away, make a copy, and mail it back immediately. After a week, phone the company or committee offering the scholarship to confirm receipt. Though they won't give you any clues as to how you stack up, they should be able to tell you if they received the application or not.

Financial need

Most scholarships are at least a little dependent on financial need. You'll probably have to submit a general outline of your income and expenses, and in some cases they may even request your income tax return. If you're Watching Your Money, this part of the application will be a breeze. You can submit your monthly sheet along with a summary of what the numbers translate into for a whole year. Don't lie on this part of the application – they can ask for the scholarship back if they find out you misrepresented your financial situation. But don't be worried if your circumstances change after you apply. There's a difference between getting a great new job with a good income and having intentionally recorded a far lower salary than you were making at the time of application. You may still have to let them know about your salary increase though, so check your paperwork.

Essays

Many scholarships require an essay, or at least a letter outlining your background, educational experience, volunteer commitments, etc. Unless you're applying for an English scholarship, your writing doesn't have to be exceptional, just grammatically correct, with no spelling errors. For help writing this essay, you can visit the financial services office, or if your school has a writing centre they can offer assistance as well. Check with friends who might be willing to give you a hand drafting or editing your submission. The beauty of today's computer technology is that you can save all your essays and simply recycle them. Make a copy, update it, target it to the new scholarship, and you've just saved yourself hours of work.

If a scholarship requires an essay, much of your competition will immediately be weeded out. Writing an essay can seem like a big investment, but scholarships requiring essays probably have fewer applicants, so your chances are better.

Generally there are two kinds of essays. The first is a personal essay where you describe yourself and your background. It's the PG-rated story of your life, and the easiest kind to write. Be confident but not boastful. Follow the word count and formatting guidelines and you'll be fine. The second kind of essay is the topical essay. You might be asked to write an essay on a topic of your choice, or to answer a question posed by the scholarship committee, like, "What has been the greatest contribution to humankind in the past twenty years?" or, "What impact have plastics had on today's medical industry?" Whatever the question, if you treat this like a regular school paper, you should be able to finish it in one all-nighter. Use a few recent periodical references and have a strong thesis.

Just as you save essays you write for scholarships, don't forget to save any papers you've written for classes. You never know when you might be able to recycle one for a scholarship application.

Proofread

Proofread everything in your application package carefully. If you forget to fill in a single question or check off the appropriate box, your application could be dismissed on a technicality. Also, there's nothing people hate more than form letters that contain the company name or other personalized information from the last letter you sent. Proofread everything you send out to ensure that if your mail merge program suffers a lapse, you've checked the letter for accuracy.

Most underrated scholarship

The winner of the most underrated scholarship trophy is the As Prime Minister Award offered by Magna International Inc. Full-time students submit a 2,500-word essay answering the question, "If you were the Prime Minister of Canada, what political vision would you offer to improve our living standards?" Fifty respondents each receive an all-expenses-paid trip to Toronto to present their papers, as well as $500 cash. Ten finalists receive $10,000 each and a guaranteed well-paying summer job with Magna International Inc. The winner receives another $10,000 and a full year's paid internship.

Why do I think this scholarship is underrated? Because even with the amazing rewards, just 1,000 students apply each year. You've got a one in twenty chance of getting $500 and a trip to Toronto. Every single Political Science, History, Communications, and English student in Canada should apply for this award. Political Science and History students have the obvious advantage of being well versed in political knowledge. Communications and English majors have the superior writing skills that can give them a competitive edge.

It's pathetic that every single student in these studies doesn't apply for this scholarship. So of course, I never did. Each year I swore I would, and I even came up with a few good ideas. I never made the time. I assumed the essays that won would be incredibly brilliant and flawlessly written, but when I finally read the winning essays one year (they're published in a book), I realized I absolutely could have had a good shot at winning.

You've got no ideas on how to improve our country? I sincerely doubt it. You're a drama/science/mathematics student, not a writer? The 2001 winner was a biochemistry student. If you can't write, have a friend who can proof review your submission. I used to proof my friends' essays in exchange for chocolate and Coca-Cola. I knew it was a long paper if a friend showed up with a case of Coke instead of a bottle.

Go to www.asprimeminister.com and start drafting your essay today. If I can write 65,000 words, you can write 2,500. E-mail me and I'll proof it for you.

Expert advice:

The University of Saskatchewan offers the following advice for scholarship applicants everywhere:

1. **Complete the application in full and follow directions.** Many students fail to read the entire award listing and application. You can give yourself a competitive advantage by carefully reading the directions. Ensure that you submit all documentation required. Do not supply things that are not requested. If a question does not apply to you, note that on the application form – do not leave it blank.

2. **Apply only if you are eligible.** Read all of the eligibility criteria and directions carefully. Ensure that you are eligible before you apply.

3. **Give concrete examples of community and school involvement as well as leadership activities.** Concrete examples illustrate your points more effectively than abstract examples. Awards administrators need to see real evidence that you meet the criteria for the scholarship or bursary.

4. **Neatness matters!** Make a photocopy of the application form and use it as a working draft. Print legibly and with care. Proofread the entire application.

5. **Develop a portfolio of your accomplishments to date.** This will assist you in identifying your strengths and preparing your application. Give a copy of your resumé to the people who are writing letters of recommendation for you. They may be able to integrate some of your accomplishments into their letters.

6. **Send a thank you note to those who have written letters of recommendation on your behalf.**

7. **Be attentive to deadlines.** You are responsible for ensuring that all parts of your application arrive on time – this includes supporting documentation such as letters of reference, lists of activities, transcripts, etc.

8. **Request help when you need it.**

9. **Have a backup plan and make certain your application gets where it needs to go.** Before sending the application ensure that it is properly addressed. Make a copy of the entire package and keep it on file – if your application gets lost you will be able to reproduce it quickly. Attach all pages securely together. Pieces of your application may get separated unless they are clearly identified, so it is a good idea to write your name on each page of the application.

10. **Remember your awards application represents you!** Preparing a neat, accurate, and complete application reflects your skills and abilities. Submit the best application you can.

Reference letters

During your university career you'll probably find a time when you need to submit a reference, or referral, letter. It might be for a scholarship, a job, or program admission. Whatever the reason, getting that letter can be a daunting task.

Cultivate connections. Who can write you a reference letter? Often the person or organization requesting the letter will tell you who should write it. They might specify that it should be written by a teacher, personal friend, supervisor, or co-worker. If you know someone who could write you a good reference letter, ensure you keep a strong connection. If you only know each other through school or work, you might lose touch when one of you leaves, but their reference would still be useful. Keep each other updated, even if just through e-mail, when you change jobs, programs, phone numbers, etc.

Time is of the essence. The day you receive a scholarship application package and see it requires a reference letter, find someone you can ask for one. Don't wait until the last minute to try to track down an old employer, or ask a professor busy with mid-terms. A good rule of thumb is to make the request at least two weeks before you need the letter returned.

Simplicity is key. When asking someone to write you a reference letter, make their task as easy as possible. Give them a copy of what it is you're applying for so they can target their comments to the criteria. A professor might request to see your transcripts before writing a letter, so make sure you have copies on hand. You may find the person you ask will simply want you to write the letter for them to review and make any changes they'd like. If this happens, don't go overboard with your praise – it might look suspicious. Your reference will probably add one or two more glowing remarks, then sign it.

Keep a record. Keep copies of reference letters. You might be able to reuse them for other applications. You might also use the wording as a start for a reference from another manager/friend/instructor years down the road.

Know your qualifications. No matter how insignificant it is or how selfish your motives, write down every activity you do, and keep an ongoing list. Did your mom force you to hand out gifts and face paint at her company's kids' Christmas party? That counts as volunteering. Do you live at home and occasionally babysit your little brother? You're committed to the values of a strong family. Do you work part-time during the school year? Congratulations, you're adept at multi-tasking, have exceptional time management skills, your organizational abilities are unequalled, and you're building a foundation for your career. Examine your life to the smallest detail and find the spin that will make your application stand out. For more ideas, see the sidebar from www.scholarshipscanada.com.

Scholarship scams

A discussion about scholarships wouldn't be complete if I didn't include a section on scholarship scams. Unfortunately they do exist, and they can hurt many students. The following information is provided by *FinAid! The SmartStudent Guide to Financial Aid* at www.finaid.org:

Scholarships that never materialize. Many scams encourage you to send them money up front, but provide little or nothing in exchange.

Scholarships for profit. This scam looks just like a real scholarship program, but requires an application fee. The typical scam receives 5,000 to 10,000 applications and charges fees of $5 to $35. These scams can afford to pay out a $1,000 scholarship or two and still pocket a hefty profit, if they happen to award any scholarships at all.

The advance-fee loan. This scam offers you an unusually low-interest educational loan, with the requirement that you pay a fee before you receive the loan. When you pay the money, the promised loan never materializes. Real educational loans deduct the fees from the disbursement check. They never require an up-front fee when you submit the application. If the loan is not issued by a bank or other recognized lender, it is probably a scam.

www.scholarshipscanada.com

Awards: Were you the student of the month, student of the year? Did you receive an award for your extracurricular activities?

Clubs: What clubs at school were you involved in? Were you in any school plays? Did you write for the school paper or yearbook? Were you involved with a religious youth group?

Co-op jobs: Where did you work? What did you do? What did you learn?

International exchanges: Did you travel abroad during school to study or volunteer? What did you learn about the culture?

Part-time jobs: Were you a cashier or clerk, babysitter, delivery person, courier, waiter, lawn care worker, camp counsellor, painter, etc.? Even if you had a really menial job that you hated, include it.

Projects: Did you work on any large projects that you are particularly proud of?

Scholastic achievement: Did you get high marks? What was your average? Were you on the honour list? Which subject(s) do you excel in?

School associations: Were you involved with your school music council or athletic association? Were you a student representative for the parent-teachers association?

Sports: What was your position on the school team? Were you the captain, co-captain, or manager? What skills did you learn?

Student government: Were you the president, secretary, treasurer, vice-president, class representative, or grade representative?

Volunteer work at school: Were you a tutor? Coach's assistant? Office helper? Library assistant? Teacher's assistant? Technical support?

Volunteer work out of school: Local hospital? Local public school? Local organization? Government office? Community newspaper? Sports team? Daycare centre? Nursing home? Describe your duties and state what you learned as a result of these experiences.

(Reprinted with permission of scholarshipscanada.com)

The scholarship prize. This scam tells you that you've won a college scholarship worth thousands of dollars, but requires that you pay a "disbursement" or "redemption" fee or the taxes before they can release your prize. If someone says you've won a prize and you don't remember entering the contest or submitting an application, be suspicious.

The guaranteed scholarship search service. Beware of scholarship matching services that guarantee you'll win a scholarship or they'll refund your money. They may simply pocket your money and disappear, or if they do send you a report of matching scholarships, you'll find it extremely difficult to qualify for a refund.

Free seminar. You may receive a letter advertising a free financial aid seminar or "interviews" for financial assistance. Sometimes the seminars provide some useful information, but often they are cleverly disguised sales pitches for financial aid consulting services, investment products, scholarship matching services, and overpriced student loans.

Protect yourself

Don't become a victim of scholarship scams. Follow these rules to identify a scam:

- If you must pay money to get money, it might be a scam.
- If it sounds too good to be true, it probably is.
- Spend the time, not the money.
- Never invest more than a postage stamp to get information about scholarships.
- Nobody can guarantee that you'll win a scholarship.
- Legitimate scholarship foundations do not charge application fees.
- If you're suspicious of an offer, it's usually with good reason.

Baby, I got the money

You landed a scholarship – what now? First, send a thank you note. It may help you get the scholarship again next year, and it's good etiquette. Second, keep a record of all the scholarships you receive. Your first $3,000 of scholarship money is not considered taxable income, but anything over that is. Ensure you include it on your tax return.

And finally, read the fine print. Most scholarships have rules regarding their use. If you drop out of school you may have to repay the scholarship, even though your tuition is not refunded. You may also have to repay a scholarship if your financial situation improves dramatically (if you receive a windfall of money) or if your grades plummet. You could also have to repay your scholarship if you break school rules – if you're caught cheating or doing some other very bad thing.

One more thing

Target the scholarships you apply for. If you don't meet the qualifications you might not want to bother applying, especially if it's a complex application. But if you think you might just get it even though you're not the perfect candidate, fill out the application and ship it. Don't pin your future on this form of free money. Whatever you get from scholarships is a great bonus, but even if you're brilliant, or a top athlete, you still might find the rejection letter in your mailbox from the scholarship committee.

CHAPTER FOUR
Get a Job ... Get Three Jobs

Unless you've managed to land a bunch of scholarships or find a generous benefactor, if you want to pay for school without going into debt, you've got to work for it.

I didn't think much about holding one or two jobs while I was in school. But I frequently met students who didn't work at all during the school year. And while a rare few were getting by on their summer earnings alone, the vast majority of them were living off loans.

For some students, working while going to school may not be an option. If you're a medical student, or in a faculty where forty hours of class and lab time is the norm, you might not have time to work between classes and studying. That's why it's so important to consider workload when choosing a program.

You must earn income to have any hope of graduating without debt. Working full-time during the summer and part-time during the school year is essential to getting out of school with as little debt as possible. Any income, no matter how small, will help you minimize your debt. If you can only work weekends, but can fit in two ten-hour shifts, do it. At $10 an hour, that's $800 a month. If your living expenses are $900 a month, that weekend job cuts your shortfall to $100. If you take out a loan to cover the shortfall, one school year's living expenses will only cost you $800. Instead, students often give up trying to find any income, and will take out a student loan for the whole $7,200.

Improve your employability

In some fields, grades are god. Employers want the top students and will recruit based on transcripts. But like most students, you may find after leaving school that employers aren't interested in your marks. They're interested in your experience and capability. Having graduated with a B-ish average, I thought I would be penalized by prospective employers for the time spent working instead of studying. Now I wish I had worked more, and studied less!

I did skip a lot of classes, and I did write papers the morning they were due. But so do thousands of students, and not because they're busy working, but because they're busy partying. I found university enlightening, but often classes required for my degree emphasized memorizing minute details of communications theory that I've yet to use, and certainly can't remember anyway. The real lessons of university were critical thinking skills, broader understanding of context, and the honing of my communication skills. I didn't learn those skills by staying up all night reading obscure texts I forgot the moment after I walked out of an exam.

Balancing school and work honed my multi-tasking and organizational skills to a fine art. I can handle a lot of pressure. Deadlines, multiple projects, and never-ending to do lists don't faze me a bit. As an example, while writing this book I worked full-time, renovated my first home, threw parties, travelled, and continued to freelance. I might have even sat down to watch television, once. I developed my skills of time management and stress management while in university. These skills landed me my current job, where the interruptions are constant.

How did I find the stamina? I always knew there was an end in sight. By working part-time during the year, I could relax and hold just one full-time job in the summer. One year I worked a little less during the school year, and had to hold a full-time job and a part-time one during the summer. The sixty-hour workweeks were brutal, but having periods of high pressure makes the relaxing time seem so much more valuable.

Studies show that students who work during school do experience a drop in their grades. It's true that working definitely decreased my studying time and my grades did suffer a bit. But not one prospective employer ever asked to see my transcripts. That said, if you're a borderline student, working too much might cause you to flunk out of school, defeating the whole purpose of working. If you're in this situation, you're going to have to find a happy medium between work and school, consider choosing another program you might be more suited for, or get that loan.

Landing a summer job your friends will be jealous of

The summer job is your best chance for earning cash to live off of during the school year, or at least pay for some if not all of your tuition, fees, and books. During the summer you can work full-time, and even hold a part-time job too, if you're motivated. You'll have more hours, and make a better salary, than you probably will at your part-time job during the school year. There are a few ways to ensure you get the best summer job – one that you'll enjoy, that will pay well, and that everyone in your faculty will be jealous of.

Classifieds suck – better job hunting

It's all about who you know, some people complain. So what's wrong with that? Get out there and start knowing people! Let people know you're looking for a job. I've had a few jobs that I learned of through word of mouth, not through a job posting. If you make a good contact in your industry, keep in touch. Send them the occasional e-mail, and when it comes time for you to find a job, let them know you're looking. They just might know someone who knows someone who's looking for a summer student.

Keith is a manager at a construction shop, and is always looking for good labourers, especially those who want to make a career of it. They rarely bother placing ads because enough people take the initiative to drop off their resumés that they don't ever need to pay for an ad.

So how do you network? It's not as sleazy a process as you might think. Networking is just about getting to know people with whom you can build career-based relationships. Correspond with other students, professors, old employers or co-workers, and people you meet at conferences. By keeping in touch with people you can hear about unadvertised job openings, new positions, and gather information about how an organization works. As an alumni working in my field, I frequently meet with students to talk to them about the industry, their prospects, and different companies. It was awkward at first, but now networking really comes naturally. I remember the people who gave me guidance and advice on my career, and I like to think I'm helping others find their niche, too.

In the spring of 1999, Derek was looking for a full-time summer job in Winnipeg. The following school year would be his last, and he was trying to avoid student loans or borrowing money from his parents. "When no one called about my resumés, I moved home to help my dad on the farm. My grandparents lived in the town nearby and often came out to visit us. My grandpa worked as a pilot truck driver on a sealcoating crew, a highway construction crew. The work is seasonal, going from May to mid-September. Each year the crew hires new people to start as flagmen, as crew members either are promoted to other crews or leave for a full-time job closer to home. Grandpa put me in contact with his foreman, who gave me an interview."

Derek aced the interview, and three days later landed a job with the company, though on a different crew than his grandfather. "I've flagged with them for three summers now. I'm guaranteed a position every summer because they don't have to retrain me, and I know how to do other people's jobs. This is the perfect job for school. It's good paying, and we get a lot of overtime. A lot of taxes are taken off paycheques, which doesn't matter because I get most of it back as a refund at tax time. I have no living expenses during the summer as I live in a mobile trailer during the week and my parents' house on weekends. When school starts my first term tuition, textbooks, equipment, and a few months' rent are covered."

Derek is grateful for his grandpa's help. He's continued on in school, and the money from the summer jobs pays much of his costs. "My grandpa was the reason I got hired for this job. Duane liked him, and the job he did on the crew. If I were not his grandson I would never have got the job, or maybe not even the interview. I'm lucky he gave me the inside tip, and such an awesome reference. School is no longer a problem for me, because of grandpa."

> **REALITY CHECK:** If you land a job interview with a company, do a little research so you can talk knowledgeably about their products or service during the interview. Your research will also help you determine if it's the kind of company you want to work for, or if you'll be selling cheap knives out of a cardboard box in industrial neighbourhoods. Be wary of commissioned jobs where they promise you buckets of cash, or where you have to purchase the product you're selling. If something smells fishy, or sounds too good to be true, it probably is.

Resumé help

Your resumé is your first impression so make sure it's a good one. There are dozens of great books on resumé and cover letter writing. My personal favourites are from the Knock 'Em Dead series: *Resumes that Knock 'Em Dead* and *Cover Letters that Knock 'Em Dead*. Written by Martin Yate, both books give you an idea of what to include in your resumé or cover letter, and what not to include. Yate includes lists of action words, strategies for dealing with employment gaps or lack of experience, and best of all, dozens of practical examples, including specific ones for many fields of work.

Your school probably has a career development office where they'll also provide free assistance or counselling.

Hire a Student (HAS) is a government-run initiative that provides career counselling, resumé writing, and interviewing skills one-on-ones and workshops through their offices across the country. The service is free, and is worth looking into, especially when designing your resumé. This service is available in both large and small cities, though the jobs and assistance they can offer are sometimes limited in smaller centres.

Online job hunting

The newspaper is the last place you should look for a summer job. Most job hunting can be done from the comfort of your bedroom with just a computer and Internet connection.

School Career Site: Most schools have a career services department that posts the jobs online. As a student you can usually access these jobs for free.

Government Services: The Human Resources Development Centre of Canada runs Job Bank (http://www.jobbank.gc.ca) an online job posting database.

Company Web sites: Are there specific companies you're interested in working for? Find their Web site and look for a Careers section. If you don't see summer or part-time jobs posted, write to the Human Resources department and inquire about opportunities.

Better interviewing

You've got an interview, now it's your chance to impress the interviewer and prove that you're the right person for the job. While many people dread interviews, if you feel and act confident, you'll interview better, and improve your chances of getting the offer.

Dress well. If it's an office job, wear your nicest suit, even if you know the dress code is casual. If you're applying for a job at a mall, a fast food restaurant, or somewhere with a young workforce, dressing well might mean clean, tailored jeans and a pressed shirt.

Brush your teeth. Get a haircut. Wear makeup. Take a breath mint. Sit up straight. A job interview isn't supposed to be a beauty contest, but studies have proven that attractive people find it easier to land jobs. Present yourself as attractively as possible (avoiding miniskirts and mullets).

Show your personality. Make light jokes where appropriate, smile, and make eye contact.

Take your time. Many people rush through interviews, saying the first thing that comes to mind after each question. Most interviewers will start the interview by telling you to feel free to think about your answers. Even if you don't need to, take a good pause once or twice before answering – it'll show you're taking them seriously.

Listen. If the interviewer asks, "What experience can you bring to this position?" recite your experience, and end with, "I really feel these experiences have put me in a unique position to understand this job." Repeat their key words, restate their questions occasionally, and show that you are really listening to them, not just worrying about what you're going to say.

Pay attention. Remember the interviewer's name, and anyone else's you're introduced to. Send a personalized thank you note to anyone involved in the interview. If a secretary greeted you, remember his or her name and use it as you leave!

For more job interviewing techniques, and for lists of popular interview questions, check out your local library.

Be your own boss

Working doesn't necessarily mean working for someone else. Many students start their own businesses while still in school, as a summer job, or part-time during the year. A great resource site is www.realm.net, the online version of the Canadian magazine, *Realm*. Here you'll find information about many different careers, and while the magazine is targeted towards graduates, there are plenty of articles about entrepreneurial opportunities for students.

Got a great idea for a business, but don't know what to do with it? The first thing to do is create a business plan. Your business plan is a detailed overview of the business you want to start, from a description of the product or service, to research on your market, to expected costs and profits. If you're selling a product, where will you buy it? What will it cost you to make it? How many employees do you need, and where will you find them? What makes your service unique? What people are likely to become your customers? What expenses will you have? How much money do you expect to make? Your business plan will answer all these questions and more. Once you have a draft ready, you can approach the Business Development Bank of Canada, your provincial business development office, or an entrepreneurship office at your school. You'll receive free assistance in perfecting your business plan, as well as in finding the financing you need to start your business.

There is funding available for student-run businesses through government and bank programs. One of the government programs is the Student Business Loan program, available in Nunavut, British Columbia, Yukon Territory, Northwest Territories, Alberta, Saskatchewan, Manitoba, Quebec, and Newfoundland. Similar provincial programs are available to students in other provinces.

To be eligible for the Student Business Loan program you must meet the following criteria:

- Be a returning student.
- Be between the ages of fifteen and thirty.
- You cannot hold another full-time summer job.
- You must work at least thirty to forty hours a week on your business.
- Your business must provide either a product or a service.
- Your business must be privately owned and be run by yourself (and partners, if applicable) independently.
- You must submit a formal business plan.

Student Business Loans are available on a first-come, first-served basis. To apply, visit www.bdc.ca.

YouthBusiness.com

YouthBusiness.com is part of the Canadian Youth Business Foundation, which provides mentor programs and start-up loans. At www.YouthBusiness.com you'll find many resources designed to educate, inspire, and assist you in starting your own business. The Web site offers guidance on creating a business plan, finding financing, overviews of business law, and forums where you can chat with other young entrepreneurs.

Before you say yes

You've researched, applied, and interviewed for a job, and get the call saying they want to make you an offer. Your first instinct will be to accept right away, but don't do it! Ask if you can give them a call back the next day, as you have another opportunity you are considering. This will give you time to evaluate whether this is the right job for you, and it makes the employer think you're more in demand that you really are, which is a great tool for negotiating a salary.

They offered you the job, so what do you have think about? Plenty. There are four important questions to answer before you accept an offer:

- Is the job something I can do, and want to do?
- Will the job further my career?
- How much will I make?
- How much will I spend?

1. **Is the job something I can do, and want to do?**
   One summer I landed what I thought was a great marketing job with a local magazine. Dressed in my best suit I started my first day not in the office as I expected, but at a desk with just some paper and a telephone. Turns out the job was not so much "marketing" as it was "telemarketing." I don't do sales, and I hated cold-calling people to try to get them to buy ads in one of the magazine's off-

shoot publications. I stuck it out until I found a better job, and it was the one time in my career I didn't care about leaving on short notice and burning bridges.

W5 recently ran a documentary about students working in the sex industry to pay for school. Students worked as strippers, sex phone operators, and even escorts to make big money fast. While holding a job like that may be damaging to your reputation, health, or safety, it's a personal decision, and not one anyone has any right to condemn. Just make sure you're comfortable with your job, and you want to do it. If you want to pay your bills by stripping, or working as a bouncer at a seedy club, as long as you're okay with it, it's your decision.

Now for the disclaimer. I definitely held jobs I didn't want and stuck with them anyway. During my last semester in school I worked as a photocopier operator in a technical oil and gas library. Doesn't that sound exciting? The title was literal. I spent each shift photocopying books, stamping them with copyrights, and mailing them off to buyers. I stood in front of an archaic machine – flip the page, copy, flip the page, copy – for hours on end. The mind-numbing boredom of it was excruciating. I kept the job for two reasons. First, the pay was good, and second, it worked around my class schedule. I had to put in a certain number of hours a week, but how I worked that out was up to me. I worked early mornings, afternoons, and evenings, whatever I could fit in.

The job was something I didn't want to do, but I could do it and the schedule and money made it attractive. If you can't find a job that meets all of your requirements, you may have to lower your standards.

2. Will the job further my career?

As I found early on in my career, and faced again after graduation, some jobs you'll be offered will pay well for dull work, while others will pay poorly for awesome work. Often, your financial situation will determine which job you'll accept. If you have a little room to manoeuvre, always go for the job with better opportunities.

The summer after my first semester of school I was faced with a difficult decision. I had an offer from the Calgary Zoo to work as a human resources assistant, writing company manuals and assisting in event organization. The $10 an hour wage they were offering sounded great, until I found out what other students in my class were making serving tables at trendy chain restaurants. Some of them were raking in $20 an hour or more in tips alone. Their working conditions were more difficult; to make a forty-hour workweek, they worked split shifts and every weekend. It was time to choose money or experience, and I chose experience. My career goal was to become a communications or writing professional, and I wanted to get a head start on the other students in my field. It worked. Every summer job following was in my field, and each paid more than the last.

I'm not slamming servers or any other non-career related job. I definitely had my share of them. Working in the service industry develops superior customer service, communication, and leadership skills, as well as godlike levels of patience. Played right, experience like this can still be to your advantage.

3. How much will I make?

I hated finding great job postings that didn't state a salary. I was a university student, and money and time were two things I didn't have enough of, so why waste either one? It was frustrating to write a cover letter, hand deliver the resumé, and skip class to go to the interview, only to find out I'd make more money bagging groceries. I always kept a minimum wage in mind, and it never failed to surprise me when I'd be offered slave wages for a job requiring experience, education, and unpaid overtime or extensive travel. If you want a fourth-year student with three summers of career-related experience, you should be willing to pay for it.

Don't be afraid to ask about salary, even when being called for an initial interview. If the employer isn't up front about the salary, it's probably ridiculously low. Be bold but polite with the person calling. I would say, "I'm excited about interviewing for this position, as it looks like a great opportunity to develop my skills. However, I noticed there wasn't a salary posted. Could you tell me what range you're offering?" I had a few people refuse to tell me, and when the question arose at the end of the interview, I usually found out why they didn't want to tell me over the phone. My father-in-law, Roman, always says, "If you pay peanuts, you get monkeys." It's not a perfect analogy (do monkeys even like peanuts?), but Roman's right – you get what you pay for.

4. **How much will I spend?**

Remember the first question? If you hate your job, you'll be miserable. And when you're miserable, it can affect question 4, how much you'll be spending. The telemarketing job I had was the longest, and most expensive, two weeks of my employment history. Every lunch hour I'd eat at expensive restaurants and shop the trendy neighbourhood, just to feel better about the day. But even if you love your job, it can still be destructive to your wallet. There are many things that will affect your income.

Transportation

Is there a bus stop nearby? Or will you need a car to get to and from work? Will a car be required for any part of the job? Will you be reimbursed for travel expenses? What does parking cost?

Clothes

Is it casual or formal business wear? Does your wardrobe need a few additions, or a major overhaul? If you need a uniform, does the company provide it? What does the uniform cost, and what does it cost to replace it?

Lunch

Does everyone in the office go out for lunch, or do they bring a lunch? If your co-workers eat at full-service restaurants every day, you'll be tempted to as well. At their incomes, they may be able to afford it, but you can't. Even buying fast food every day for lunch hurts – at $5 a day, that's $100 a month. Brown bagging it costs as little as $2 a day, a $40 expense instead. If everyone eats out every day, do you really have the willpower or desire to stay at your desk and be the odd man out?

Neighbourhood

Is the job close to a mall? Or is it in an industrial park? Is there a walking path or park nearby? The location of your job can cause money woes. When I worked downtown I'd end up wandering along shopping avenues at noon, buying $8 lunches and picking up useless sale items along the way. The summer I worked at the zoo was a penny-pincher's dream. I'd bring a lunch and walk around, sitting on the grass to eat, watching the animals, sometimes the visitors, and sometimes just reading. My co-workers did the same, and I didn't feel pressured or stressed at all.

On-campus employment

Getting a job on campus might be a great idea, especially if you live on or close to campus. However, evaluate your options carefully. During my first year of university I worked at the coffee shop in the student centre. The location was convenient and the hours weren't too bad. I thought my wage was okay, until I found out I could make $2 an hour more at a coffee shop a kilometre away, and not have to serve my classmates and professors. Some campus jobs are much better than others, in terms of both the work and the pay. Apply at the library, parking service, registrar's office, or recreation centre, but skip the fast food court.

The Great Co-op Scam

I referred to my school's co-op program as the Great Co-op Scam. To participate in the co-op program, you had to take an extra year to graduate and you were committed to full-time studies or a co-op job each semester. I wouldn't have had the option of taking less than a full course load each semester and would have lost the part-time salary that paid my bills.

Also, for the privilege of being accepted into a work placement, you had to pay the school a $325 fee per term! For some of the jobs they had posted, that was a week's wages. And during a work term, you still had to pay student union, health, and dental fees, whereas students working regular summer jobs didn't have to.

Despite the downside, I decided to talk to someone in the co-op office anyway. I knew the co-op program had better jobs than the regular summer job postings – they kept them password protected on the Web site for co-op students only. I talked to an advisor, who reviewed the details of the two summer jobs I had already completed, and declared they would be accepted for credit. All I had to do was pay $650!

I can almost understand charging the fee when the co-op office works with companies to develop and post jobs, help students apply for them, and sometimes arrange the interviewing. But they wanted to charge the exact same fee when they hadn't done anything? Like I said – scam!

I didn't join the co-op program, but I did still want to see the jobs. I had a friend in the program, and begged him to e-mail me the Communications postings, which he did. I applied for one, explaining in my cover letter that, while I wasn't a co-op student, I felt I had the qualifications they were looking for. They felt so too, and I got the job – the best paying one yet. It was devious, I know, but it worked.

I don't see the value of the co-op program. If you're clueless about interviewing, resumé writing, and other job search related skills, the regular career services people are more than happy to give you a hand. You could also visit your city's Hire a Student office. The co-op program's only apparent value is giving you access to better jobs. But if you follow the techniques I mentioned earlier, you'll likely find those jobs yourself, saving you hundreds of dollars, and a lot of time.

But just because I don't think the program is a good deal doesn't mean you shouldn't try it. Thousands of students enrol in co-op programs every year, and find the experience rewarding and valuable. Kari is a graduate of the University of Calgary's Communications program. She enrolled in co-op in her first year, and landed positions in her field each semester. None of the four positions was ever advertised to non-co-op students. "As a student in Communication Studies, my favourite joke is always that I'm learning how to better communicate: 'would you like fries with that?' Truth of the matter is, I don't find the joke very funny. Though I love my degree, I often worry that it qualifies me to do absolutely nothing, and that terrifies me. Entering into the co-op program was the only way I saw to fight that fear."

Kari was definitely frustrated by some aspects of the program. "I found the co-op process to be exceedingly tedious, with many hoops to jump during the acceptance process. Hours of required and redundant workshops meant to educate me in the resumé writing and interviewing processes served only to repeat past high school lessons. In fact, the entire ordeal was enough to make me stop long before I had started, but then the thoughts of bad summer jobs and working in coffee shops for the rest of my life made my stomach turn enough to force me through the rest of the hoops.

"Once in the co-op program, the experience improved. My first posting was with a not-for-profit organization that was in desperate need of additional staff. I was given several tasks and was consequently able to learn at a rapid rate while adding several items to my portfolio. My subsequent posting was with the government, and there I was able to learn a very different skill set in a very different environment. Finally, my last two postings were with an oil and gas company in their corporate communications office. Though the two previous postings gave me some work related to my degree, corporate communications gave me the ability to see several different uses for my degree within one department while being exposed to others in my field. Learning from others as well as from the position helped to better guide me in my career direction."

Was it worth it? Kari thinks so. "My university experience would not have been the same, nor as valuable, without the co-op component. I now feel I am able to enter into the workforce and quickly become a contributing member. Though the classroom education I received was complete, it was not practical for communications positions. With both the theoretical and practical experience, I know I can take on the many challenges ahead."

The perks

Remember when I said the easiest way to pay tuition is to get someone else to? Usually that's scholarships or relatives, but in a third case, your boss might be willing to shell out the bucks. I talked previously about the unclaimed scholarship myth – employer tuition is the "scholarship" they're referring to. Even if you're at a part-time job, if it's career-related, some companies will pay a portion or all of your tuition, as long as you pass. If you've never heard of this, ask your manager directly, or talk to someone in the human resources department. If they don't have the program set up, ask if they'd consider your situation.

Kevin is a nineteen-year-old electronics whiz. While he was in high school, Kevin learned about the Registered Apprenticeship Program (RAP), which allows high school students to become apprentices. "Before I was even done grade twelve I worked with a local electric company, earning money and accumulating hours towards my apprenticeship program. Once I graduated I entered the Southern Alberta Institute of Technology's electrician's program." Kevin works for ten months, and goes to school for two months. Not only does he earn good money while working, but his employer pays part of his tuition and the government pays the rest. He also qualifies for unemployment insurance during the two months he's in school. If you were wavering between choosing a trade and choosing a degree, choosing to learn a trade first could not only keep you out of debt, it could actually make you money.

Student or teacher? You can be both

If you're in your last year of a program, getting a master's or graduate degree, or are just a stellar student, you might be able to land a teaching assistant (TA) or research assistant position. If you get a formal TA position you can expect to assist one or more professors grade papers, prepare lessons, or run tutorials. Not only will you get paid but you may get course credits, and have a portion of your own tuition covered. Another interesting position is that of a research assistant. You can set your own hours, work for a prof you like, or make money working from home or an office on campus. Talk to your career office at school, or ask your favourite professors if they know of anyone who is looking for part-time help.

Work for your fellow students

Did you know your student union representatives get paid? They do! Most positions on the student union are paid, and while you may have to take time off from school if you have a high-up position, you'll add some incredible experience to your resumé. Some of the positions don't require time off, but a minimum monthly commitment of time, and you may receive an honorarium or tuition credit. Other campus programs can offer something similar. For instance, the Safewalk program at the U of C provides a safe escort when walking on campus at night, and the program volunteers receive credit towards tuition. Talk to your student union about what positions they have available, and find out what the perks are.

One more thing

Think of working your way through school as part of your education. If you can find a job related to your field, you'll gain practical experience that will impress future employers, putting you a step ahead of the other graduates. You'll also gain income you can use to pay for your tuition and living expenses, allowing you to decrease your loan needs. Trying to find career-related employment while in school could be an eye-opener for you too. If you can't find any part-time or summer jobs related to your program, will you be able to find a full-time job once you've graduated?

CHAPTER FIVE
Gimme Shelter

Finding a place to live while in school is a substantial money issue, and one of the reasons many students go into debt. This chapter will review the pros and cons of the many different types of living situations.

Big decisions

Keith and I could have kept living at home while going to school. We had the usual teenage growing pains and conflicts with our parents, but we knew they loved us and wanted the best for us. After five years of dating, we really wanted our own place and thought we could manage the cost. I had just two years of school left, Keith three, and with two incomes, it was definitely going to be easier for us than for an individual on their own. Looking back, the real mistake wasn't moving out, it was getting married.

Okay, before the relatives start calling, let me clarify. Getting married wasn't a mistake per se – we're happily married. But the wedding? Financially, it was a mistake. We refused to let our parents contribute towards the cost, wanting to do it on our own. Even with the generous cash gifts they and other relatives gave, we still spent $6,000 on the wedding above what we received. And we got married outdoors in a campground! Trust me when I say weddings are expensive.

Coincidentally, $6,000 is the amount we had to borrow for school, so our method of prioritizing expenses sometimes wasn't perfect. A drive-through wedding with a bad Elvis impersonator would have been much more affordable, and definitely as memorable, but not quite what I grew up fantasizing about.

So for the last few years of school, we decided to live on our own. We looked at apartments, finding the ones in our price range tiny and far from school and work. We considered renting a house with friends, but worried about the stress of finding renters, and ensuring everyone pitched in with housework and bills. Plus, as newlyweds we weren't thrilled about the idea of living with other people. We moved out to avoid that! In the end, we decided to rent a basement suite. We began and ended our search with the student housing list, a listing of apartments, basement suites, and rooms for rent the student union printed weekly.

We found our dream place with the Starke family. It was a 650 square foot walkout with a full kitchen, crawl space for storage, big windows, and a separate entrance. It was in a nice neighbourhood, we were a short bus ride to school, and had off-street parking. We were thrilled with the place. The Starkes owned the house, and their nanny had lived in the suite for nine years until their kids grew into teenagers. They wanted to rent the suite to a student for a few years, and they priced it low hoping to attract a number of applicants so they could choose someone responsible, and help the student out. When they chose us, we were ecstatic. We lived with the Starkes for two and a half years, finally moving out once we had graduated and bought our own home.

We had really wanted to move out as soon as we started school, but knew it would be a costly decision. Moving out isn't a decision you can make without serious thought, and it could mean the difference between graduating debt-free or graduating in the hole.

Hotel Mom and Dad

The vast majority of our friends lived at home for most, if not all, of their education. For some, it was their parents' only financial contribution to their education. And it is that – trust me, your parents want you out. Your mom wants your bedroom for guests and your dad is thinking about knocking down the wall to build an entertainment room. But most parents are happy to allow you to stay while going to school, so take advantage of their generosity.

Maybe you can't stand your parents. You're twenty, and they freak out if you're not home by midnight. They're on your back about your grades, your girlfriend, your car, and your job. The only upside is that you're living rent-free while you attend school.

Sound familiar? For many students who choose to live at home during school, home conditions aren't ideal. While on campus and with your friends you feel mature, responsible, and important, while at home, you're treated like a ten-year-old.

> **REALITY CHECK:** Your parents might not mind if you stay out all hours, or they may think it's "their roof, their rules" and establish a midnight curfew. Whatever type of parents you have, you need to have a conversation about house rules. Now that you're out of high school they'll probably be more relaxed, but then again, they might not be. Talk about guidelines for chores, groceries, privacy, entertaining guests, and anything else you think may be an issue. Then follow them. If you've agreed to the conditions your parents have set, stick to them. If you can live at home, you need to recognize it's a sweet deal, and ensure it doesn't end! Don't forget to show your family respect. You might think a curfew for a twenty-three-year-old is ridiculous, but if the dog barks his head off when you try to sneak in at 3 a.m., it disrupts the whole house.

Expert advice

Justine has lived in all kinds of situations including living on her own, with multiple roommates, and with her parents (and still enjoys a great relationship with them). She graduated from Simon Fraser University debt-free thanks to her experiences as a co-op student. She is now the editor of www.iamnext.com, a Web community full of information and tips on student concerns like relationships, career, and spirituality. Here are her ideas for maintaining your sanity while living at home:

Create a life for yourself outside of home. Living at home doesn't have to mean social suicide. Meet new friends in your classes or in the many campus clubs and activities you should join. Hang out at other venues: restaurants, coffee shops, the campus pub, clubs, parks, or someone else's party. When you do have people over, be respectful and keep the noise level to a minimum.

Don't ignore your family. Chances are, you'll be on a different schedule than your parents most days anyway. Spend enough time with them so they aren't frustrated with only seeing the back of you walking out the door all the time. Be respectful. Don't treat home like a hotel or your parents like the front desk people. Appreciate them and try not to take them for granted. Take them out for dessert once in a blue moon.

Communicate. Sit down to discuss expectations, like you would with a roommate, about curfew, alcohol, room privacy, food, having friends and guests over for visits, phone usage, study time, and your contribution to the house (financial or chores).

Set boundaries. Establishing boundaries, both time and space, will help you maintain your independence. Decorate your room like an apartment or dorm room. Get your own phone.

Enjoy it! Remind yourself often of all the little perks: you don't have to pack and move, pay for rent or laundry, attempt cooking, or share your bathroom. You might even have access to a car and have a quiet study spot. Besides, you won't be living with your parents for the rest of your life!

If you're attending a hometown school, how long can you handle living at home before you really do lose your mind? Try setting a goal for yourself, like, "I will move out when I have $4,000 saved," or, "I will move out when I find inexpensive housing and good roommates." Set achievable goals that will help you succeed at living on your own.

Friends and family

Whether you go to a school in your city or not, living at home may not be an option. Your parents may have kicked you out the door at eighteen, or you may have serious conflicts with them that can't be resolved. Can you lean on friends and family for help? Do you have any friends still living at home you could stay with? How about relatives in the city? While you will still contribute rent and grocery money, you may be able to find a place to stay for less money than renting on your own or sharing a house with people you don't know.

Scott is a student at St. Mary's University in Halifax. His family home is in Jeddore, a one-hour drive from school. Driving to and from campus each day didn't seem feasible, in terms of time and money. But living in the city wasn't cheap, either. So Scott approached his grandparents who lived just a short distance from school. For three years of his four-year program, Scott lived in a room in his grandparents' house. While he didn't pay rent, he did contribute to the grocery bill, help out around the house, and provide companionship to his grandparents. "I certainly didn't get to live the party life while living with Nanny and Granddad, but I did save a lot of money. I had meals made for me every day, and a quiet place to study. I was very lucky."

If you find a place to stay with friends or family, show them the same respect you would a landlord. Pay your rent on time, clean up after yourself, respect their privacy, and show your gratitude.

SINK OR SWIM

Living with strangers

If you can't find a place to stay at home or with friends or family, realize that your costs are going to go way up. You'll need to approach finding a place to live strategically. Don't put off thinking about moving until the day that your parents change the locks. If you know you're going to move, plan ahead. The best and cheapest places get rented early, both on- and off-campus.

Living in residence

Did you ever watch the television show *Felicity*? Their dorm rooms were awesome. Spacious, funky, unique – and totally unlike reality. In the real world dorms are tiny, contain only the bare necessities, and are identical to every other closet on campus.

Living in residence is an experience like no other. Living in a house with parents and siblings is very different from living in a building full of other adults. In a dorm you may have to share a room, something most of us haven't ever done, except on family vacations. Your dorm-mates have their own ideas of "normal life" that are probably very different from yours. Something as simple as the frequency or timing of showers could cause major problems.

Most students enjoy the community aspect of living in a dorm. Lifelong friendships are developed, and dramas unfold daily. In dorms, activities are planned, and residents are encouraged to compete against other floors or buildings. Parties, sports, or other events are scheduled. It's a great way to get involved, especially if you're from out of town and don't have friends already in the city.

Though I never lived in residence, some of my friends did, and they have both positive and negative stories. Lots of people means lots of drama!

Residence buildings are generally co-ed, meaning the floors or buildings are co-ed, not the rooms. You can get single or double rooms, and at some schools, three- or four-person rooms. Residence buildings might be restricted to students in certain faculties, or in specific years of their programs. Residences usually include:

- Furnished rooms (bed, dresser or shelf, bookcase, and desk)
- Meal plans
- Lounges with televisions
- Laundry facilities
- Mail service
- Reserved parking
- Telephone service
- Internet access

At many schools, student housing, or residence, is available for much cheaper than living off-campus. If you're considering moving into or out of rez, log onto your school's Web site for details of their residence costs. Here's a breakdown for two universities:

At the University of Manitoba, a double room and the food plan in the cheapest building is $3,560 for the year, which is the eight months of fall and winter studies. The food plan portion is $1,700, and can be used at food service locations around campus. Your total cost is approximately $445 a month. Not bad right? Now compare that with the University of Calgary. A double room in the cheapest building is $1,455 for the year. The basic food plan is $1,935 while the 'Hearty' plan is $3,170. The total cost of the cheapest living arrangement is $3,390, or $423 a month. The total cost of room and board buying the more expensive food plan is $4,845, or $605 a month.

Does this mean if you're a big eater you have to buy the expensive food plan? No. Depending on the type of food plan, the starvation plan might be okay, even if you are a big eater. Some plans charge by a flat point system, where a six-course meal is worth the same as a bowl of cereal. Others, like the University of Calgary, are by dollar value. Smart selections can stretch your food plan farther, especially if you avoid buying junk food on your plan when you could get it at the grocery store much cheaper. Think about your eating style. Are you happy with on-the-go food like fruit, granola bars, or sandwiches? Or does every meal have to be a square, home-cooked one?

If you're considering rez, check out their rule book before you make a commitment. Things like the food plan, regulations about food and refrigerators in dorms, parking, and telephone privileges may make or break the deal for you. Opting out of the food plan is not permitted, so check out your residence options carefully. The food plan or policies (no refrigerators allowed) may make rez much more expensive than living with roommates off-campus. Don't forget other expenses, though. Utilities are included in rez, while you may have to pay part of that bill elsewhere.

Did you notice in all my examples I quoted the rates for double rooms? That's because they're cheaper than single rooms, by about a grand a year. Considering most dorm rooms are less than 150 square feet (probably smaller than your bedroom at home), if you really have to have your own bedroom, rez might not be your first choice. Single rooms are more in-demand, and first-year students aren't high up on the priority list for those rooms. If you get a single, you could be looking at $550 to $700 a month for shelter and food.

> **REALITY CHECK:** If you're going to a school in your city but can't live at home, rez probably isn't the answer. Not only will you likely have last priority on the sign-up list, you may not be able to live there during the summer months. Some schools will allow you to live in rez during the summer, but check before you commit.

More about rez

Living in rez isn't all about the rent and food costs. If you live on campus, you can probably land a job there too, limiting your transportation costs to the occasional bus or taxi trip. Because your room comes fully furnished, you won't have to pay to purchase furniture and other items.

Residence can be a bonding experience for many students, giving them an opportunity to create relationships with people they wouldn't normally meet. Living in rez can also give you opportunities to develop your leadership skills if you choose to accept a paid or volunteer position there. At some institutions you can even receive credit for residence employment. Many students in residence participate in fundraising events and other charitable initiatives.

Leah is twenty-three years old, with a Bachelor of Arts, English major from Saint Mary's University. She has great memories of living in rez. "Although residence is the main reason I have debt, it was the best decision I ever made. I learned about life in residence much more than I would have at home. I tried both living at home and residence and living in residence really made the most of my time in university. It helped me to learn to focus and work in a team. Believe me, eighteen females living on a floor together 24-7, with only three phones and three bathrooms, wasn't always a picnic, but it taught me life lessons. I am now a training specialist for Staples. I am responsible for the training of approximately two hundred people in three locations in Canada and the U.S. I think my time in residence, especially as a residence advisor, taught me the skills I needed to excel at my job today."

Hate the lunatic you're sharing your room with? In most dorms there are advisors with the responsibility of assisting you in working through personal issues with others in the dorm, including your roommate. If things don't work out, you can try to switch, but it isn't always easy.

REALITY CHECK: There's pretty much only one way to get ahead of the game when applying for residence. Apply early. That's it. Most schools will let you apply for a spot before you know you've been accepted to the school itself, so the day you send away your application for the school, send it for rez, too. If you have top of your class grades you might have a better chance of getting in. Some residences offer preferred status to students they really want in their school.

Off-campus housing

You've decided to live off-campus, or had the decision made for you. Where will you live? You can stay in a one-bedroom apartment or basement suite, rent a two-bedroom place with a friend, or find roommates for a larger place. Some apartments come furnished, but don't pay more for a place because of that. Armed with just $100, a Saturday of garage sale and thrift store shopping, and asking friends and family for their unused furniture, will fill any apartment with the basic stuff for sitting, eating, and sleeping.

> **REALITY CHECK:** Usually students who live in residence move back home for the summers. If you moved to another city to go to school and didn't choose to live in rez, or couldn't get in, moving back home each summer is probably a really bad idea. It's usually much cheaper to stay in your school city and work there. Besides the travelling costs, you've got a bigger problem – your living arrangements. If you're renting, you may not be able to get an eight-month lease and will either have to pay for the rent even when you're not living there in the summer, or find someone willing to sublet. Finding someone to sublet your place for just four months will be incredibly difficult. You'll likely have to take less money for the rent, and you'll have to find somewhere to store your stuff, or leave it and hope it doesn't get ruined or stolen.

Student housing lists

Thank you, student housing list! Over the years, the U of C student housing list has helped me and many of my friends find inexpensive housing close to campus. A free service to renters, landlords pay a small fee to list their rental property. You don't have to be a student to check out this list – it's available on the Internet and in the student union office. If your school has a list, it's the first place you should look when renting. Once you've graduated you can still use it to find affordable housing. If your school doesn't have a list like this, check with your city. They likely have a department devoted to affordable housing and will be able to provide something similar.

The Single Life

The cost of single bedroom apartments is astronomical in some cities, and quite reasonable in others. In Calgary, you can usually find a one-bedroom apartment or basement suite, including utilities, for around $550 a month. Halifax is a little cheaper, Vancouver a little more expensive. Deciding to live on your own is an expensive choice. If you can't afford it without going into debt, don't do it. Re-evaluate what your money is going towards. If you give up your car, can you afford your own place?

"But I need to live alone." You want privacy, and you want your own place. I can definitely understand that. There's a reason most people give up the roommate thing once they're out of school. But remember your commitment to yourself to get an education without threatening your future financial plans. You knew this wouldn't be easy, and this is one of the really hard choices. You might not find it too difficult to pack a lunch instead of buying one every day, but living with roommates is probably a sacrifice you really don't want to make. Do you need to live alone? Or do you just want to?

While living by yourself means total control, it also means total responsibility. There's no one to rack up the bills, but no one there to help pay them. There's no companionship, but no late-night parties while you're trying to study, either.

Roomies

If you can't afford a single apartment by yourself (few students can), sharing a place with roommates is a great way to spend less on shelter and other bills, while still having a larger place with better amenities than a single apartment might have. There are positive and negative elements of living with roommates, so keep this in mind when deciding to make the move into a house full of people.

Roommates can be expected to contribute to:

- Groceries

- Meal preparation
- Utilities
- Phone bills
- Cleaning

Roommates will also contribute to:

- Fights
- Messiness
- Noise

Living with other students can help you cut costs in other areas too. Can you carpool to class or work? Can they give you a ride once in awhile to save you the hour-long bus trip? If one roommate has a car, you can take advantage of grocery sales and stock up, saving the taxi fare or a stressful bus trip.

When considering a place, identify what's included in terms of house bills, rent, and any responsibility for repairs. If it's a house full of people you're moving in with, try to meet them all before you make your final decision. Ask about security – are there a lot of guests coming in and out of the house? Can you install a lock on your room if you want? Are house rules established, written or unwritten?

Organizing a house

There are significant benefits to being the person organizing roommates to rent a place. Because you're essentially the house manager, you can choose the place, set the rules, and find the roommates. You also set the rent. If you're renting a house with four rooms for $900 a month, you could theoretically charge $300 a month per person, and live rent-free yourself. It's not scamming the other renters because you're the one responsible for finding new roommates when one leaves, you keep the house running, bills paid, and you deal with the landlord.

Keep in mind that setting rent high might result in wealthier roommates, but it might also scare off some great matches. Setting it too low could result in too many applications, and could leave you in trouble for money if you underestimated housing costs.

Finding great roommates

Finding people interested in renting a room usually isn't the hardest part. You can find roommates or try to become one by looking at a student housing list, putting up posters around campus, or asking around. The hardest part is choosing the right roommates. You might be looking for people who want to keep to themselves, or you might want to create a party household. Make sure you're clear with prospective roommates about what the house rules will be, and what they will be expected to contribute.

Ask questions to ensure their lifestyle is a fit with yours and anyone else in the house:

- Do they have pets, or can they live with yours?
- Do they smoke, drink, or do drugs?
- Are they early risers or night owls?
- Have they ever lived with roommates?
- What is their schedule like – do they work, go to school, or just party all the time?
- Where does their income come from?
- What are their expectations for household chores?

Don't get burned

If you're the person organizing the house, ensure you have a good system for collecting money and getting bills paid, and make sure it's fair. If one roommate is making long distance calls on the house phone, he should pay those charges – it shouldn't be split evenly. Some houses share the grocery bill, while others designate portions of the fridge and a cupboard or two for each person. There's no right or wrong way, as long as everyone is happy that it's fair.

To protect yourself and other roommates, everyone should sign a lease, either for the semester or the year, to ensure you some protection against roomies who disappear overnight without paying their rent. You can ask that they sign a House Rules document, where you can outline:

- The date rent money is due
- The date bill money is due
- Which bills and what percentage of them the roommate will be responsible for
- Quiet hours
- Overnight guest policy
- No pets allowed, certain pets okay, who cleans up after them, who lets them out, etc.
- Grounds for immediate eviction (theft, breaking too many rules, violence)
- Parking, laundry, telephone, and garage privileges

You can find sample roommate agreement forms online. A good one is available at www.roommateservice.com/roomate_agreement_form.

Dealing with landlords

As a tenant, you have certain rights. You are protected by your provincial government, and you can log onto their Web site for more information, or check the phone book for an information line. For some general guidelines, keep reading.

Get everything in writing, with a signature. If your landlord is supposed to shampoo the carpets before you move in, get it in writing. Don't be confrontational, but insist on it. Most landlords won't do anything they don't have to, and if it's not in writing, they don't have to.

Watch your money. When you move in, you often have to pay first and last month's rent, as well as a damage deposit. Did you know your landlord has to pay you interest (set by the government) on your last month's rent? Make sure he does! And get it in writing.

Record all damage. Damage deposits on rental properties are standard, especially for students. Make sure you write up a list of all damage before you move in, and have the landlord sign it. Include everything, no matter how small. If the landlord later tries to blame a big carpet stain on you, even though it was there when you moved in, he could keep your entire damage deposit as money towards new wall-to-wall carpeting. What if your landlord gives you permission to paint the walls a new colour? I hate to repeat myself, but get it in writing! Otherwise you'll get dinged for a new paint job when you leave, even if you made the place look like a *House Beautiful* spread.

Fill your house

It's moving day. You face blank walls, threadbare carpet, and nothing to sit on. Don't despair!

The first thing you should do is call your local Welcome Wagon. Don't give me that look – they're a great resource! Check www.welcomewagon.ca for a contact in your area, then call them and let them know where you live and that you're new to the area. They'll send a representative to your house, and for a half-hour of your time they'll load you up with free stuff, including coupons for free food at local grocery stores, money saving coupons, free cups, pens, medicine, toothbrushes – tons of stuff provided at no charge by local businesses. If you end up using these businesses, let them know you heard about them through the Welcome Wagon. It encourages them to continue handing out the freebies.

Furniture

Your student apartment isn't going to be in a photo shoot for *Style at Home* magazine, so don't get caught up in creating a page out of an IKEA catalogue. Following the Good Enough for Now principle, you can furnish your apartment for next to nothing by shopping at garage sales, thrift shops, and asking for contributions from friends and family.

Buy things cheap. How long do you want it to last, anyway? When you're out of school you'll probably be moving to a bigger apartment, or into a house, where the things you had in school just won't cut it.

Throughout university, we had the most hideous brown, flowered couch. It came with the basement suite and it was comfortable, but it really was an eyesore. Every once in awhile I'd look around for a cooler couch, cruising IKEA, the Brick, or Sears. I would always find great couches, but usually they cost $500 or more. Keith would convince me to wait it out, that we'd buy a new couch once we graduated. Now I'm glad we waited. The couch that would have fit perfectly in our small suite would look silly in our new house, and we've chosen lounge chairs for the living room anyway. A nearly new couch would have been stuck in the basement, sold, or given to friends.

Always check to see if you can purchase furniture floor models for cheap. You're going to ding them moving them anyway, so you might as well get a deal on something that's already scratched. Just don't scratch it yourself at the store. If you get busted, you'll pay full price, and may be charged with property damage!

The basics

You'll need a few basic services, including heat, electricity, water, and a telephone. You'll probably also want cable, and maybe even Internet access.

Utilities

Getting your utilities is just a matter of contacting your local utility office. I'm sure you know the tips and tricks on how to lower that bill – keep the heat low, turn out lights, and minimize your use of high energy devices (dishwashers, washing machines) when possible. Experts suggest you adjust your thermostat by no more than three degrees at any time. Turning the heat down to 15°C at night and up to 20°C for the day means you actually use more energy than turning it down to 17°C for the night. Heating the house back up to 20°C takes more energy than keeping the temperature more consistent. For other ideas, call your utility company. They may have a free informational brochure they can send you with more ideas on how to trim this expense.

Telephone

Telephone service is a basic you can't live without. But are you sure you want a traditional telephone? Some cell phone companies now offer plans with limited daytime minutes, unlimited evening and weekend minutes, per second billing, and no contracts to sign. If you don't use the phone much during the day, you'll have the benefit of owning a cell phone without having to pay two phone bills. Check the plan carefully before you commit, and never sign a long-term contract. Getting out of it is next to impossible. And don't buy into a contract because you get a free phone. No-contract cell phones are super cheap, and the savings on a no-contract plan usually make up for the free phone.

The downside of a cell phone is that paying for voice-mail is usually mandatory. You have to have a way to receive messages when you're not picking up. You don't want to miss out on a job interview or extra shifts at work because no one could get in touch with you. If you buy a cell phone, try to talk the service provider into throwing in the voice-mail service for free, either forever or for the first year. If you have a traditional phone, you're probably better off buying an answering machine. You can get a new one for under $20 pretty much anywhere.

Stocking up

Stocking a kitchen doesn't have to be expensive. For food preparation, you'll need a few kitchen basics, including cutlery, dishes, glasses, knives, mixing bowls, cutting boards, can opener, frying pan, pots, and baking dishes. Many of these items can be found at dollar stores or thrift shops for next to nothing. Don't forget to help yourself to free items whenever possible, like plastic cutlery at fast food joints.

Beyond white walls

If the prison cell look just doesn't cut it, here are some inexpensive ways to decorate your place, college style:

Grab a paintbrush. With permission from the landlord, painting is a cheap way to brighten your place. Check your local paint and hardware stores for mis-tinted paints. The selection is usually quite nice, and you can get a lot for very little.

Put up a few posters. Movie rental stores always have large, full-colour posters lying around in a box, free for anyone interested. Grab a few for movies you liked, and check indie stores for really funky ones.

Nurture your green thumb. Plants can be obtained just by cutting slips from other plants, and potting them in dollar store planters. All you need is a little light and water – expensive fertilizers aren't required. For a little nostalgia, plant a small bean in a clear plastic cup!

Become an art collector. Create a tacky art display by buying bad artwork from garage sales for just a few bucks, and encourage your friends to add to your collection.

Display everything! Display CD covers in cheap clip-frames. Display interesting scarves or T-shirts found in thrift shops, or buy a foreign magazine and frame the ads (Japanese magazines are available for less than $10 and have the most out-of-this-world English ads). Pick up frames at yard sales. Even if the artwork in it hits the trash, you can reuse the frame, painting it if necessary.

Create your own art. Marcel Duchamp made a living displaying and selling "readymades" in the early 1900s – things like a urinal, a bicycle wheel, and a shovel. Find something interesting, mount it, and call it art!

Protect your junk

You got a place, decorated it, and moved in everything you own. Now you need to protect it all. Every day you hear stories about people who have had house fires or robberies, and lost everything. In the case of natural disasters, sometimes Red Cross steps in to help, or family members or a local business will start a collection. Most of the time, whatever money is raised is only enough to help the family buy food and clothes to last a few weeks, or rent a hotel room until they can find another place.

What would happen to you if the place you live in burned down? Where would you go? How could you afford to replace your things? Could you afford to continue to go to school?

Thinking about insurance is something every student needs to do, even if you're living at home. Your parents may not have adequate insurance, or they may have none at all. Talk to them about it, and find out what coverage they have.

Whether you live in a basement suite, apartment, or house, in case of a fire or burglary, the landlord may have insurance on the property, but he likely won't have coverage for contents, which means your possessions. You'll need to take out tenant insurance. While all insurance feels like a waste of money when you don't need it, when you do, you'll be glad it's there. And tenant insurance is one of the cheapest insurance premiums you'll pay.

Depending on your coverage needs, tenant insurance will run you between $100 and $200 a year. If you're sharing a house it will cost more, but you'll have more people to share the expense. Try to find the best rate possible from a reputable company. If you have a vehicle, check with your auto insurance company. They may give you a discount for having both policies with them. But call around and get a few quotes before committing. Sometimes the discount rate is far more than the rate at house insurance only companies.

One more thing

Whether you want a great place to party or a quiet spot to study, your living situation is an important part of your school experience. Living at home while attending school is the best option and can free up some of your income for the finer things in life. If living at home isn't in your future, weigh your decision carefully. You'll be stuck with it for at least a year, and it could cost you more than you accounted for.

CHAPTER SIX
All-Consuming Consumerism

This chapter is about all the things students spend money on – mandatory things like textbooks, expensive things like computers, sanity-saving things like travel, and a host of little things, including gifts, pets, and bank services. In short, it's about consumerism, both the good and the bad.

Reduce, reuse, recycle

Reducing consumption, reusing items, and recycling. It isn't just a mantra drilled into our heads as children, along with, "Only you can prevent forest fires!" Saving the environment while saving money – what could be wrong with that?

Reducing consumption is a common theme in this book because in doing so you'll also reduce costs. Do you drink bottled water? Consider buying a jug with a water filter for your fridge and filling a travel bottle with water instead. Drink pop by the can? Switch to two-litre bottles, or water instead. Turn out lights when you leave a room for long periods of time, or switch to more energy efficient light bulbs. Grab a sweater instead of turning up the thermostat. Reuse items until they're absolutely worn out, not just not perfect anymore.

Here are a few easy ways to reduce your consumption and save money:

- If you pay bills online, keep the return envelope included with your bills to use for something else (make sure you cross out any addresses and Canada Post code lines).
- Don't waste money on sticky notes when scrap paper will do. Save all paper with some white space on it for that purpose.
- Use less shampoo and detergent when washing your hair and clothes. It'll still do the job for less money and with less waste.
- Forgo the expensive cleaners. Vinegar and water works just as well for a tenth of the cost.
- Reuse plastic grocery store bags. At most stores each bag will get you a few cents off your bill.
- Make your own wrapping paper or give gifts in dollar store gift bags. Skip the expensive Hallmark wrap.
- Practice "precycling" by buying products that use the least amount of packaging or contain recycled materials.
- Read the newspaper online, or at your school library.

If you're interested in finding more ways to save money and reduce consumption, there are thousands of hints available in *The Tightwad Gazette*, available from your local library. Here you'll find tips on how to save money in every facet of life, from food to household repairs to beauty tips. Amy Dacyczyn, the author, is the frugal guru – there isn't a frugal living tip she misses in her book.

In many small cities, and even some big ones, local recycling depots allow you to drop off your recycling as well as unwanted household items, including furniture, bikes, and golf clubs. The items people leave are often fine to take and use. I've seen great bikes dropped off simply because the chain is broken! The repair cost is minor, but these days we worship the gods of bigger and better, so people would rather buy something brand new. Check the phone book to see if your city or community has this set up.

Why you shouldn't photocopy books (and why you will)

The cost of textbooks can be a real burden, especially since it's hard to plan for it. Some semesters you'll spend $100, others you'll spend $500 – it all depends on your courses and your instructors.

Other than just not buying textbooks, the cheapest way to get your books is to photocopy them, and it's a method many students are driven to by the high cost. Walk through any student photocopy centre and you'll see students blatantly copying the pages of textbooks, stacks of coins next to the machine.

You shouldn't photocopy your textbooks. It cheats the author and publisher out of income they deserve for their work, it's unethical, and it's illegal. But thousands of students do it anyway. They borrow the book from the library, a friend, or a classmate, copy it, and give it back. They may even buy it from the bookstore only to return it after copying. A $0.05 a page photocopying place can allow a student to copy an entire book for less than $15, and in under an hour. If you only need a few chapters, it's even cheaper, and quicker. Some bookstores are wising up to this practice, requiring you to provide a reason for returning the book, and they keep track of how many books you bring back.

I don't condone photocopying books, but I will admit that I did it. When it came right down to it, I could either spend $95 on a textbook for the science requirement course I didn't give a damn about, or I could pay my health care bill. I hated doing it. As a writer, I know how much work goes into creating a book, and how very little of the money from the sale of each book the writer actually receives. But if publishers don't want students finding ways around paying full price, they need to look at their pricing. Producing a hardcover edition in full colour isn't the only option. They could find less expensive printing methods and utilize cheaper paper.

Professors need to share the blame, too. They hold the most power over your textbook dollars and they're losing touch with reality. They assign four or five textbooks for one class, choose the most expensive ones on the market, and assign new editions each year, ensuring you can't buy your texts from the used bookstore.

Profs have a choice. They can choose to assign ten texts, or just one. They can choose texts that are inexpensive or available in the used bookstore. Ever taken a class where the prof taught right out of the textbook, reading the lesson word for word? I did, and whenever I recognized this, I returned the book right away, and made sure I attended every class. Other profs would assign three textbooks, never mention them in class, then only test on the textbook material! Unfortunately, there seems to be no logic to the thinking of professors on this issue. That's why I've included a tear-out letter for you to sign and give to your professors. Photocopy the letter and give it to your friends. If professors start receiving enough of these letters, or any comments about the affordability of their required reading, maybe they'll think twice about assigning $400 in textbooks for a $350 class. Want a more anonymous way of providing your feedback to your profs? Ask your student newspaper to print this letter as a wake-up call to the school.

Dear Professor,

Did you know that the average student debt load after graduation is almost $20,000?

As a student, I'm trying my best to fund my education without going into debt. Books are a rising expense, and I would like to ask you to assist me in keeping my education affordable. Did you know many students never buy the required textbooks for their courses? The cost of textbooks can be prohibitive, and can mean the difference between buying groceries or visiting the food bank. Students are resorting to purchasing textbooks at exam time only, returning them after the exam. Others are photocopying textbooks from classmates.

One of the ways you can help is by reducing the number of textbooks you assign as required reading. When you're creating your required reading lists for your courses, please keep in mind the financial situation of your students. The fewer books you can assign, the better. If a text is not really needed, please mark it as suggested reading, not required. Also, if you have a choice between two equally good textbooks, please assign the less expensive one – even small savings add up quickly.

By purchasing used textbooks, I can save up to half the cost of new ones. To ensure used textbooks are available, please assign the same book for a few years in a row. I realize many texts come out with new editions each year, but sometimes very little has changed. If you could provide supplementary material on the new information, or perhaps teach that in class, it would save your students thousands of dollars.

Thank you for taking the time to read my plea. I know you value education, and I appreciate your help in making it affordable for everyone.

Save money on books

So you're going to be honest and buy your textbooks. Here's how to save some coin while ensuring you get the book learning you need:

Buy your books on time. If you buy your books too early, you may find you don't need them but it's too late to return them. If you buy them too late, you won't find copies in the used bookstore. Buy your books as close as possible to the start of the semester to ensure you can return them if you don't need them, but can still find used copies.

Shop around. Don't blindly trust the campus bookstore to have the best price. If the used bookstore carries the book, you'll definitely get a better price there. If it's a new book, or the used bookstore is out, check Chapters. You'd be surprised at the titles they carry, or can have shipped at no charge, and often they have better prices.

Split the cost. If you can work out a schedule for sharing a text with a classmate, do so. Borrow the books on a week by week basis, or form a study group to go over the text and course material together.

Return for refund. If you only need a few chapters of a book, why pay for the whole thing? Buy the text, make notes from it, and return it within the time frame for a refund.

Check your local library. Your library might have copies of your required reading, especially for English, Political Science, Art, and Canadian Studies courses.

Selling Used Books

Selling your books when a course is over is a good way to raise funds for the next semester's book buying needs.

Try the used bookstore first. While most new bookstores have buy back plans, you'll probably be offered far less than what you'd make selling your books at the used bookstore.

Check your course outlines. Don't sell books you can use again in another course.

Ask around. If you know a few people in your program you may be able to sell your books directly to another student, cutting out the consignment fee the used bookstore will charge.

Even if you think you'll want your books for future reference when you're working full-time, think about selling them anyway. You'll have the cash you need now, and you can buy the books later if you discover you do need them. You'll only be losing a few bucks, and that loss will be deferred until you're in a better financial situation. Though I kept about six books from my courses, I've never needed to refer to them. You'll probably experience the same thing.

Join the 21ˢᵗ century - get a computer

Like textbooks, computer access while in school is mandatory. The majority of students will need a half-decent computer to type papers or projects. Once we moved out on our own, we didn't have the money to buy a computer, so we used the computer labs on campus. It was hard to find a lab with open computers, and I used to stand in the line-up glaring at the students playing on their Hotmail accounts for hours. Didn't they have jobs or classes to go to? If your school has numerous computers available, try to get by using those for your assignments before running out and buying your own.

If you do enough computer work and live far enough away from campus that only having computer access at school is a real hardship, you'll probably need to buy a computer.

Buying used

You don't have to own the best computer out there. If you're at all computer savvy and can solve some problems yourself, a used computer might be the way to go. Just make sure it works first. Don't pay for anything you haven't plugged in and tested. Look for ads around campus near the end of the school year, or check your telephone book for used computer dealers.

If you work for a big company, contact your IT department to see if they have an employee purchase program. Many companies offer employees the chance to purchase old computers that work fine but aren't up to the high demands of complex programs and daily use.

Buying new

If you're a total computer novice, you might want to buy a new computer. But just because it's an expensive purchase, don't think of this as an investment. Computers are rendered obsolete far too quickly for you to want to spend any serious money on them. Don't forget, you're not buying for the future, you just need something Good Enough For Now.

Unless you're in a Computer Science or design program where you need complex and expensive hardware, go for the bare minimum. A hard drive, monitor, keyboard, modem and a mouse – forgo the speakers or the printer. You can usually plug $5 earphones into your computer instead of paying $100 for computer speakers. To make buying your own printer a good decision, you'd have to print tens of thousands of pages. Local copy shops can almost always print your work for pennies a page, about the same as you'd pay when using ink cartridges and without having to incur the cost of the printer.

Split the cost

If you have roommates, it's a great idea to share a computer – financially. Logistically, it just won't work. When three of you have papers due the next day, who gets the computer? How do you determine who pays for the computer, repairs, or upgrades? When a roommate leaves, how are they compensated for their part of the purchase? Sharing the cost of a computer probably just won't work.

Computer perks

There are other benefits to having a personal computer with Internet access. Having a computer at home allows you to complete assignments and do research at any hour of the day, which makes Clock Watching much easier. You can also chat with friends online, saving on long distance bills, find free programs, enter contests, send away for free stuff, and download coupons. The Internet is a great tool for scoring freebies or finding information on just about anything quickly.

Internet access

Internet access is almost a necessity for students these days. Registration, class notes, and even courses are available online, usually more quickly and less expensively than through traditional services. You can get cheap (though slow) access from your school or another community program. If you decide to sign up for high-speed service, expect to pay between $35 and $50 a month. Installation charges range from $75 to $150, but you don't need to pay that. Call around to check prices, and ask for the installation and first three months of service free. Even if they don't have the promotion on when you call, they'll usually give you that deal anyway. You just have to ask.

Software

Like downloading music or photocopying books, copying software is illegal. Maybe if a simple word processing program produced by a multi-billion dollar company didn't cost in the hundreds of dollars, pirating wouldn't exist. If you're going to respect legality and purchase your software, shop around. While my campus computer store was supposed to offer low student pricing, it consistently charged $25 to $150 more for programs than a nearby big box office supply store. If you're buying a new computer, see if you can get the software that you need thrown in for free. If you've haggled a killer deal on the price though, it probably won't fly.

Something for nothing

Something a lot of students miss out on is how much stuff they can get for free – an easy way to cut your expenses! You can score tons of free stuff every day, just by actively looking for opportunities.

Go to a trade show. You can explore an interest, and take home pens, magnets, books, notepads, mouse pads, coupons, and even clothes.

Need some cheap T-shirts for working out or bumming around the house? You can snag totally free T-shirts at www.petrix.com/shirt/.

Free computers disks are handed out frequently on campus. Delete the stuff on them, and you've got a free disk.

The first week of classes is a great time to grab student saver packs from your student union or school bookstore. These packs usually come with free samples of shampoo, razors, deodorant, and other items. Take a bunch. The people giving them out usually don't care how many you snag.

Visit the Web sites of your favourite hair care, beauty, or other products. Many have a sample request form you can fill out to receive free goodies.

There are truckloads of free stuff given away online. While applying for these offers guarantees you'll end up on junk mail and spam lists, you will get lots of free samples, and sometimes even full-size products, all for a little typing time.

Free stuff online

http://www.canuckcash.ca/
http://www.canadianfreestuff.com/
http://www.geocities.com/totallyfreecanadianstuff/index.html

Free stuff is good, but there is a time to avoid it – when it's not really free. Be wary of free with purchase offers. You may end up paying more because you're buying a more expensive product than you normally would, just to get the freebie.

Gift-giving guilt

Birthdays, graduations, housewarmings, Christmas – every month, you need to buy gifts for people. Need? Did I say that? Let me correct that statement. You WANT to buy gifts for people.

Gift-giving is a time-honoured tradition, and one loaded with equal amounts of love and guilt.

During university, I dreaded Christmas. I'd resolve to shop early, whittle down the list of gift-exchanges, and not go overboard. But most years my resolve went out the window when the Christmas carols began (approximately Labour Day). I would shop early. I'd buy everyone a gift in October. Then I'd find better stuff in November and buy that, too. I loved finding the perfect thing for everyone on my list. Or the perfect five things.

Another problem I faced was guilt shopping. Having bummed off friends and family during the year, I wanted to shower them with gifts at Christmas, even though I really didn't have the money. I'd splurge, and dread the January Visa bill. I never thought about the flip side – I was causing guilt for those I gave gifts to. They felt badly that I spent so much on them when they knew I didn't have the money. I'm facing that problem now, as friends try to give us expensive gifts to thank us for our help during the year. It makes me feel badly to know they'll be hurting financially because of their gift. But how do you say no graciously?

In looking for advice on dealing with gift-giving pressure on the Internet, I stumbled across a Web site that offered suggestions on how to save money when shopping. One of the tips blew me away. It encouraged readers to get a holiday job to ensure they could afford the gifts they wanted to give. I was shocked. Is this what Christmas is about? What do you think your loved ones want, a better gift or more time with you? If you think it's the former, find new friends!

Don't spend what you don't have. Most of us make our list then spend whatever it takes to finish it. Instead, we should be deciding how much money we have to spend first, then creating a list that matches our available funds. If you have the willpower, shop all year when great items go on sale. If not, take cash out of the bank and do your shopping quickly.

Be it birthdays or Christmas, here are some ways to cut gift-giving costs:

Trim your list. We exchanged gifts with close friends at Christmas for years, until one year I decided we weren't going to do it anymore. It had become so mechanical. They'd tell us what DVD they wanted, we'd make a request, and we'd swing by and drop the gifts off at each other's homes, usually not even coming in long enough to take off our shoes. It wasn't personal, and it wasn't in the spirit of Christmas.

Start a new tradition. If you have numerous family members to buy for, see if they'd be interested in a gift exchange, or in drawing names for gifts. If you're a family of bargain hunters, why not exchange gifts on Boxing Day after a late dinner? You can buy your gifts that morning and wrap them in the afternoon (with Christmas wrap bought at 75% off).

Make your gifts. You might be crafty, and decide to create handmade soaps for everyone on your list. If you're a computer whiz, build a family Web site where members can post photos, events, and messages. Not super creative? Buy calendars for family members and write in everyone's birthdays, anniversaries, and special family get-togethers.

Be realistic. My brother admitted he had considered an expensive gift for me, one he thought I would really like. Then he thought to himself, "If Sarah had $75 to spend on anything she wanted, would this be it?" He knew the answer was no. I have so many personal wants that he couldn't possibly find the thing I would have wanted to spend that money on. So why spend so much? Instead, he could find something for far less that I'd probably enjoy even more than the $75 item.

Receive graciously. Don't buy $5 gifts for everyone on your list, but drop hints that you want an Xbox. Appreciate the thought behind the gifts you receive and don't judge them on their monetary value.

Wrap it up in style. Dollar stores are great places to find inexpensive wrapping paper or gift bags, but your least expensive alternative is to buy a large roll of white or brown craft paper from an art supply store. Decorate it yourself, or just leave it plain.

Reckoning with the tax man

While in school, you probably won't have to pay much tax on your income. Even if you work full-time in the summer and part-time during the school year, your tuition is tax deductible, and you receive credit for the months you're attending school. This will probably bring your income down close to the basic personal tax-free limit.

Buy Nothing Christmas

Buy Nothing Christmas is a campaign created by the Canadian Mennonites. While the cause is a religious one (the intent is really to get back to the meaning of Christmas, celebrating Christ's birth), it doesn't mean non-religious people can't learn from the initiative. Here are some of their free or inexpensive gift-ideas:

- Create coupons for a massage, spring cleaning, child-minding, manicure, etc.
- Create a menu of various culinary delights and have the gift recipient choose one of the options.
- Collect meaningful photos for the gift recipient, make colour photocopies, and create a collage.
- Videotape and interview your elderly parents about childhood memories, how they met, etc., and give to siblings or children.
- Paint an empty wine bottle with non-toxic paint and fill with olive oil. Top with an oil pour spout that can be found at a gourmet cooking shop.
- Make a mixed cassette tape (or compact disc) and choose songs that make you think of that person. Under each title, explain why you chose that song.
- Make a calendar with pictures of family members.
- Buy a used book and on the inside cover explain why you chose the book for that person.

For more ideas, visit www.buynothingchristmas.org

Deductions

Above a certain amount, your income is taxable. If you can keep your income below that magic number, you won't have to pay any tax at all, and if you go over it a bit, you'll only pay very little tax. If you find yourself over the basic personal tax-free amount, even after your education credits and tuition are deducted, you can lower your taxable income even further.

Want an easy deduction? Donations are tax deductible, but only a certain percentage. For instance, if you donate $100 to charity, you'll see less than $20 of that money back at tax time. You've got the warm fuzzies, but you're $80 poorer. Want to get that deduction for nothing? If you've got clothes, furniture, books, and other used items you no longer want lying around and you don't think you can sell them (or don't have the time to), donate them to a charity, and get a tax receipt for the value of the donation.

Did you move to attend school? If you relocated more than forty kilometres to attend classes, your moving expenses are tax deductible. Save all the receipts, and ensure you only claim the allowable expenses.

> **REALITY CHECK:** You might not need to use your full tuition and education credit deductions, and if your parents are footing some of your school bill, you can transfer those credits to them as a thank you. You might want to save the benefit for yourself, though. As you progress through school, your summer and part-time earnings will probably increase as you find better jobs for higher wages. Those unused credits could come in handy in your last year or two of school to keep your income under the tax radar.

If you can't prepare your taxes yourself, most student unions provide tax preparation free of charge, or for a nominal fee, for students. Take advantage of this! As a student you're unlikely to require any complex accounting work. The guy at the one-hour tax place in the mall probably isn't going to find you any amazing tax loopholes to save you more than the cost of his fee, so using a student service is the affordable alternative. If you decide to have your taxes done professionally by an accountant, you can deduct the fees on your next return. Be sure to ask for a receipt.

Travelling on a shoestring (a.k.a. surcharge-free travel!)

So you want to see the world? If you need to take time off to do it, I recommend you take a year off before school to travel Europe, or visit Australia the year after you graduate. But travelling abroad during your school career? If you're reading this book, you probably don't have the moola needed to travel internationally.

If you're determined to travel while in school, you might be able to take advantage of the Student Work Aboard Program (SWAP), managed through Travel CUTS. SWAP takes care of the details for you, like your visas, help getting a job, and help finding a place to live. Canadians can visit countries including Britain, Ireland, Japan, Germany, Australia, South Africa, and New Zealand, among others. You'll work while you travel, earning enough money to pay for your expenses, but not really enough to save any real amount for school. You have to have some cash saved up to go, from $2,000 to $4,000 – enough for your flight and to prove you can cover your basic expenses when looking for work.

For more information on SWAP, visit their Web site at www.swap.ca where you'll find testimonials, contacts, background information, and an application package.

Get outta town

As a student, your travel plans are probably limited to visiting home, if you're living away from school. Attending a school in your city or within a few hours' drive from your family home makes it much easier to spend less money travelling. If you're living in a different province, a trip home once a year could cost you $500 or more just for the flight, even with a seat sale.

The wheels on the bus go round and round

Travelling by bus or train is a really cheap way to get where you need to go, but it frequently takes much longer than flying. Factor in travel time when you're comparing costs. If flying costs $200 more than travelling by bus but it gets you home faster and you can work a day or two extra, you might want to shell out for the plane ticket. Ask for student pricing – most road transportation companies offer great rates for students. What about sharing a ride? Your student union or campus newspaper might list ads from students looking to share a car and gas money driving to a different city over break. See what's available, or organize your own trip and put up a posting.

It's a bird, it's a plane...

For most students living more than a province or two away from home, airline travel is the only option. There are many myths surrounding airline fares. Some people mistakenly believe the only way to travel inexpensively is to buy a ticket during a seat sale. However, if you buy well ahead of time, up to seven months in advance of your flight, you'll get a pretty good fare. While you may land a seat sale fare the day before you want to fly, you'll probably only save $25 or less each way. Seat sales aren't a sure thing. Airlines only offer them when they need to boost the load factor on a plane, so the odds of you finding a seat sale fare for the flight you want on the day and time you want are pretty slim. Plus, if you've already booked and then you do find a seat sale at a way better price, you can cancel your ticket, get a credit, and book again at the better price. Check the change fee though, as it might not be worth it to change. Also, be sure you use the credit within a year or you'll lose the money.

Buy online

If you have access to the Internet, purchasing tickets online, either directly through the airline's Web site or though a service like www.travelocity.ca or www.expedia.ca, can be a good way to find cheap flights. You can spend as long as you like checking out the options, and usually save a couple of bucks off the same fare bought through a call centre or travel agent. Once you've purchased your ticket, ensure you receive your itinerary and check everything carefully right away. Call the airline immediately if you see any problems with your booking.

Get credit

Got a good book with you? Offer to be bumped off your flight. If you travel with an airline that routinely bumps passengers, show up for your flight an hour and a half early, and when you check in, let the counter attendant know you're willing to be bumped if necessary. You'll catch the next flight out, and get a credit either for the full amount or a partial amount of the flight. Either way, you'll have a good chunk of credit to help cover the flight next time.

Banking blues

Students get great deals at most financial institutions, mainly because they're hoping you'll carry an enormous balance on your credit card and pay them interest for life, or you'll feel loyal enough to eventually get your mortgage with them and pay interest for life. The big banks, and many non-traditional ones, offer free banking, no annual fee credit cards, and even higher interest rate savings accounts.

Call around to find the best deal. If they don't offer it but you like the bank's location or hours, ask for the deal anyway, letting them know who does offer that service for students. Don't choose a bank that has no bank machines, or branches you can't get to easily. You may get a million free services, but if you have to pay a one or two dollar service charge every time you withdraw cash from another bank's machine, it isn't worth it. One near campus might be your best bet, as it will remain a constant while you're in school.

Ask to have some services thrown in at no charge. The worst they can say is no. Just by asking I frequently received free overdraft protection, a valuable feature for months when your bank balance hovers near the $5 mark. Don't rely on your overdraft, though – it's not free cash, it's a high interest loan. And it really sucks to deposit your paycheque and find it only brings your balance barely above zero, the rest going to your overdraft amount.

Always pay your bills on time. Not only will you avoid service charges or penalty fees, you'll ensure you don't mess up your credit rating on that account. And check your monthly statement as soon as you get it. The banks are notorious for making errors, and you don't want to have to fight for your money months later.

> **REALITY CHECK:** Always read the fine print. Many consumer credit cards and no payment, no interest deals sound great until you read the fine print. Let's say you buy a couch on a no-interest-for-one-full-year deal. If you choose to prepay for the couch, you may have to pay at least half of the outstanding amount each time or you'll owe a service charge. Some companies state that if you don't pay off your balance when the year is up all the interest, from the date of purchase, is now due. Others even force you into a high-interest payment plan if you haven't paid the debt off in full by the time it comes due. So read the fine print – it could really cost you.

Learn the art of complaint

A letter to Famous Players complaining about the subzero temperature in the theatre and the overpriced admission landed me a free pass. Another letter to Burger King about their slow service staff at the location by work, and I scored a free lunch. Pizza Hut sent coupons, Wal-Mart sent a $25 gift certificate.

I'm a skilled complainer, and you can be, too. You don't have to get terrible service, but if you can offer suggestions for improvement, you'll usually receive the same response – free stuff. Ask for bigger fitting rooms, cleaner washrooms, faster service, and let them know you'd like to continue being a customer, but would like to see improvements made.

In my experience, sending an e-mail or calling a customer service hotline may be faster and easier than typing out a letter, but I rarely receive compensation or coupons for e-mails. 99% of the time when I send a real letter, I receive free stuff back. Take the time to type a letter, and save it as a template to use for other letters. Send it to Customer Service at the company's head office address, available on most company Web sites. Avoid sounding angry or upset, or making any demands. If you say you want a gift certificate or something else for your troubles, you usually won't get it. Instead, just take the tone of a "concerned customer wanting to help you improve your business."

Jack is a graduate who has mastered the art of returning items when in school. "I buy a lot of items online or through catalogues, and whenever I have to send something back, especially if I don't have the receipt or it's past the return date, I always include a really nice note and a secret weapon – a small, wrapped chocolate. I've returned dozens of things, from ski jackets to books, and it always works. Recently I received a donation request at work that included a small chocolate. I had to decline the request, but I was impressed that someone else out there knew my system!"

You might think it's too much trouble to complain, but think about it this way: that one letter to Wal-Mart took me just ten minutes to write, and cost me $0.50 to mail. I earned $25 for the tiny investment!

Taking care of Fluffy and Fido

Pets are great companions. They love you unconditionally, they're at your side when you're lonely, and they are a source of entertainment. And while you may have grown up with pets and really want one in your life, as a student, it's probably not feasible. Even fish are expensive, when you think about the cost of the tank, filters, heaters, tank decorations, food, medication, and then the fish!

An animal like a cat or dog is unrealistically expensive for any student who lives on his own. For instance, I recently adopted a cat from the Calgary Humane Society. They warned me to not take the responsibility lightly. Between his vet visits, pet insurance, food, toys, litter, and other miscellaneous items, Parker costs about $65 a month. Can you handle that expense? You can't just not feed the dog if you're short a bit of cash one month.

If you think you can handle the money and, of course, the responsibility of a pet, visit your local shelter. There you can talk to a volunteer about the costs of owning the pet you're thinking of adopting or buying. If it's $75 a month, save that money every month for the next year in a separate bank account. You'll not only prove you can afford an animal, but you'll also have an emergency fund in case your pet gets sick and needs special medical care.

If you decide to bring a pet into your home, check your local shelter first. Some people have the misconception that animal shelters only have older, abused animals, however they have puppies and kittens more often than you'd think. By choosing an animal from a shelter, you'll spend hundreds less than you would at a pet store, your pet's first vet visit and spaying or neutering is usually free, and you're rescuing an animal that might otherwise have been put down.

One more thing

Every decision you make concerning money impacts your quality of life now and in the future. It's often the little things that will send you into the world of loans and debt. Be smart with your money, and spend it wisely.

CHAPTER SEVEN
Making an 8:00 a.m. Class

Fresh into university, Keith bought the POS '85 Ford Escort hatchback. After a few years of driving the temperamental heap, he generously sold it to me for more than he paid for it (never underestimate the power of love). He bought a '92 GMC Sonoma and began his life's work of driving me crazy begging for money to fix it up. When we married, I sold the Escort for pennies. By that point the car was missing mirrors, the headlights were permanently glued in, and she refused to start in temperatures below a mild chill.

Just before graduating I decided to buy a car, and chose a '97 Hyundai Accent. I've had her for nearly two years, and she's been a dream car. And while it was great to have one or two cars during our university careers, it was a mistake financially. While owning one car was a necessity throughout university, owning two for even part of the term was wasteful. Giving up my POS Escort wasn't particularly enjoyable, but it did save us money.

Lose the freshman ten

Unless you live on-campus, it's unlikely you'll be able to walk to school or to work. However, when you're looking for a place to live, or a job, think about its proximity to school. Will walking be an option? What about biking?

Buying a bike for daily commuting is expensive when you compare it to the $100 bike you got from Canadian Tire as a kid. These days, outfitting yourself with a good road bike and all the extras (protection, locks, water bottle, backpack, and headlight) could cost you up to $1,000. Compared to the cost of a car though, or even the bus, a bike will pay for itself quickly.

Buy a quality bike, new or used, and not from a department store. Visit a reputable bike shop and talk to the clerk about what you'll be using the bike for.

Plan to pack and invest in a good, sturdy backpack. You may need to carry a change of clothes, books, or other items for work or school.

Protect yourself from theft. Buy a good quality lock system, but keep in mind it won't deter professional thieves. Lock your bike in a well-lit, high-traffic area. Remove the front wheel and pass the lock through the wheels, the rack, and the frame. Removing the bike seat will deter some thieves.

Buy a bucket. Ensure you have a good quality, properly fitted helmet.

Learn the rules of the road.

Rules of the road for cyclists vary from city to city. To learn the rules for your city, check out your city Web site.

Nasty public transit

Public transit in Calgary is terrible. I imagine you feel the same, regardless of where you live. The buses never seem to be on time, they're full of loud and obnoxious teenagers (we didn't behave like that, did we?), and the schedules are awful. Pretty much the only thing going for the transit system is the price. I had one bus that stopped outside my door, and it took me directly to school in twenty minutes. It took longer to drive and park, and yet I still preferred to drive. However, taking the bus didn't kill me, and while I'd still bum rides from friends or classmates whenever I could, the bus was my main source of transportation when in school. Is it an option for you?

I'm the first to admit that ride-sharing or carpooling is next to impossible. If you're going to school and working, your schedule and destinations will probably be very difficult to integrate with others to share rides. If you're determined to try it, check out www.carpool.ca, a Web site run by Commuter Connections, a non-profit society operating out of British Columbia. It's a great resource for students, as it has networks in many Canadian cities.

If you want to take public transit but none of the routes or times fit your needs, write a letter to the transit authority. If they get enough feedback they may create a new route, new stops, change the route a bit, or increase the frequency of buses. If you can find others in your area who would like the same service, ask them to call or write in their requests. The more response they see, the more likely they'll make a change.

Universal Pass

Many schools across Canada are now implementing Universal Pass systems (sometimes called U-Pass). Check your school to see if one is required. Depending on your transportation needs, a U-Pass can be a saving grace, or just another useless fee. U-Passes cost around $50 a semester, and they allow the holder unlimited city transit service. With a monthly student bus pass costing about the same, it's a great deal for students who take the bus, but not for those who don't. A U-Pass, if implemented by a school, is a mandatory fee. You pay it with your tuition, even if you don't take public transit. The service is so inconvenient it takes an hour and a half for the bus to make a ten-minute drive, so you will likely have your friends or parents drive you to school every day. However, if you live in an area where you cannot take the bus to school – you're outside the city limits, or in an area not serviced by a bus – talk to your student union. You may be able to get the fee refunded.

When to buy a car

If you're serious about graduating with as little debt as possible, the only valid reasons to own a car while in school are if you cannot get to school without one, or you lose money by not having one. How can you lose money by not having a car? Let me explain.

You're offered a job at a downtown pub. While the salary is low, the tips are great. However, your shift ends at 2 a.m., when public transit has long since shut down for the night. Your options may seem limited, but there are still three major considerations.

1. Ensure the job will cover the costs of the car, and still give you more money than a job that doesn't require one. If you make $300 a month more than you would at a place near your home or school but the car costs $400 a month, it's not worth it. $100 a month is $1,200 a year, or $4,800 over a four-year program. In some schools, that's a full year of tuition.

2. Make sure there's no other way to do it. Do any other employees live near you? Can you pitch in on gas money in exchange for a lift home? If the late nights are a rare occurrence, would $100 a month in taxi rides and a bus pass be cheaper than a car?

3. Commit to the job. If you crunch the numbers and still feel you're able to afford a car at that wage, ensure the job is long-term. Because when you leave the job, you won't want to give up the car. Suddenly you'll find yourself justifying the expense, and it's easier to live without than to have to give something up.

Wheels required

Keith began working for a stair company in his first year of university. He'd work there part-time during the school year, and full-time in the summers. He also worked part-time in the evenings on campus for Parking Services. We tried to work his schedule without a vehicle, but it just didn't happen. He worked at the stair company from 7 a.m. to 9 a.m., then went to school from 9:30 a.m. until noon. Back to the stair place for another three hours, then a few more classes. Most evenings he worked for Parking, a job which allowed him to get in a lot of studying time.

Without a car, Keith wouldn't have been able to keep the stair job, as the hour-long bus ride (for a ten-minute drive) would have kept him from working the short hours. Very few companies are as flexible with their employees, and he wanted to keep that job, the pay, and the convenient hours. He worked five hours a day that wouldn't have been possible without a vehicle, and the $60 a day, or $1,200 a month, more than paid for the cost of the car. If you're in a situation like this, get the car. But keep reading to find out how you can keep your car costs to a minimum.

REALITY CHECK: Car costs

The Canadian Automobile Association produces a Driving Costs brochure every year. For 2002, they report the average commuter spends approximately $7,500 per year for the privilege of driving a car. Their statistics are based on the average Canadian, and while your car will likely have a lower price tag, the maintenance costs might be higher. Grab a pen and paper to find out the real costs for the vehicle you're looking for, and the estimated insurance based on your driving record. Here's what my Escort cost the first year I had it:

1985 Ford Escort	Costs	Your Car Costs
Cost of car/loan	$2,000	_____
Insurance	$1,000	_____
Gas	$900	_____
Regular maintenance	$200	_____
Parking	$200	_____
Repairs	$500	_____
Registration	$50	_____
Total annual cost	$5,000	_____
Total monthly cost	**$416**	_____

If owning a car is not absolutely necessary to get you to school, the only other excuse for having a vehicle is that it gets you to work. Will the monthly cost you figured out above be covered by your job?

How to buy a car

Buying a vehicle is a big decision, and you should spend a lot of time looking for the right car. Here are a few tips to help you get the best ride for your money:

Never buy new. Ever. Buying a brand new car is a huge waste of money. If you were to buy a used car and sell it a month later, you could probably sell it for the same price that you bought it. Not so with a new car, where you'd lose $2,000 or more.

Reasons to buy new. You want a reliable car. Don't kid yourself – the money you pay for a new car is just money spent on prestige, not safety. A car a few years old that has been well maintained is no less safe than an overpriced, brand-spanking new set of wheels. Check out Transport Canada's vehicle recall database at www.tc.gc.ca/road-safety/recalls/search_e.asp and you'll see that brand new cars have lots of bugs, too. Are you going to buy a new car every year because your current vehicle isn't safe? If you ensure the car you purchase has passed a safety inspection, reliability is no excuse.

If you buy a new car, you get cash back or low-interest financing. So what? You've got a new car for $15,000 at 1% interest. How is that better than a $5,000 car at 10% interest? After three years you'll have paid $15,232 for the new car, and $5,808 for the used one. Having bought the new car, you'll now be stuck with a used car, but be over $9,000 poorer.

The family connection. Can you beg your parents for their old beater? Do you have a sibling or relative willing to sell you a car for less than it's really worth?

Do your research. Before you go browsing, research the car you're considering buying. While you're not going to be buying a Cadillac Escalade, you don't want to drive something that's going to cost more in repairs than it's worth. What you can afford is up to you, but somewhere in the $2,000 to $6,000 range will get you a decent car. You could go wandering around used car lots, and you might want to stop by one or two first to get a feel for them and the cars available, but when you get serious, you've got to be prepared. Check out www.canadiandriver.com for reviews of new and used cars, and check www.canadatrader.ca or www.megawheels.ca for price ranges. For any car that interests you, write down the vehicle details and the asking price. Compile a big list, and then start seriously looking.

Ready, set, shop!

Individual sale

Buying a car from an individual is the cheapest way to go, but you won't get the security of a big name dealership standing behind the purchase. If you're buying from an individual and you're really serious about the car (you've reviewed the paperwork, taken it for a test drive, and like the price), ensure you get a full inspection done by a certified mechanic. This is not the time to rely on free advice from dad. It usually costs about $60 for an inspection, but it can save you thousands of dollars in repairs. Don't believe the word of the seller, and don't rely on his mechanic's inspection. Get your own.

Don't want the cops seizing your car the week after you buy it? Do what's called a lien search at a registry. People sell stolen cars all the time, and if you've bought one, you're out of luck. You likely won't get your money back from the seller (he's probably left town) and the rightful owner of the vehicle gets it back. You get nothing. Also, a lien search will tell you if the car has been written off or salvaged, something you need to avoid.

Dealerships

I prefer to buy vehicles from dealerships. I know I'm paying a bit more, but I like the security of a dealership standing behind the vehicle, and I can usually negotiate a deal for not much more than buying a car from an individual. Negotiating with a used car salesman is a high-pressure situation, and I love it. Here are some tips to make your experience getting a good price on a dealership lot less painful:

Know your stuff. If you've done your research, you should be prepared with information on the car you're looking at and prices you've seen listed for private or dealership sales for that or comparable models. If you know a '98 Tracker is worth between $9,000 and $12,000 depending on the options, mileage, and condition, you won't get talked into paying more because you're ignorant of the market.

Ignore the options. One car comes with a CD player, air conditioning, and power everything. It's $1,000 more than a similar car without all the bells and whistles. What do you do? You buy the cheaper car. It's Good Enough For Now, and the extras are wants, not needs.

Conceal the truth. The salesperson will ask you what your price range is. Don't give a range. If you say $5,000 to $6,000 and you start discussing a $5,000 car, how can you negotiate a lower price? The dealer already knows you can afford $1,000 more. Instead, tell him the type of car you want and ask to see similar models. You'll already know they're in your price range.

Ask a lot of questions. Even if you don't care about the answer, asking a ton of questions about the car and the previous owner shows that you're serious, and you're not going to buy the car just because it's a cute shade of purple.

Everything's negotiable. The sticker price is not the real price. The salesperson expects to negotiate, so be prepared. You've got two strategies – offer lower than what you're willing to pay and negotiate up, or offer exactly what you're willing to pay and don't budge.

Don't shop on impulse. Promise yourself that you won't buy the first car you test drive. And don't buy a car the first time you visit a particular dealership. Even though the car may seem great, going back a day or two later will give you perspective, a chance to shop around, and show the salesperson you're not an easy mark.

Don't fall for sales tactics. If you shop around, you'll find the same tricks used over and over again to try to get people to buy cars at high prices. Some sneaky tactics include having staff pretend to be interested in the car you're looking at, or telling you someone else is coming back that night to make an offer. I actually had a salesman say to me, "I can't sell it for that price, I have to make a living. I've got three kids." It was nothing more than a pressure tactic, and I left immediately.

Look early. Give yourself time to find the right car at the right price. Some days you'll find the perfect car, but it's overpriced and the dealer won't deal. You don't want to be pressured by time, because you want to...

Be prepared to walk away. If you're not getting the treatment or the deal you want, walk away. You will find another car. The salesperson will try to keep you in his office for as long as possible. When he leaves to check your offer with the manager, they're not talking about your offer; they're talking sports. The more of your time you commit to this car, the more obligated you'll feel to sign the paperwork even though it's not the price you want. Even if you've sat in the salesman's office for two hours working out a deal, be prepared to walk away if he doesn't give you the answer you want. It will show the salesperson how serious you are, and when you return a week later and the car you haggled over is still taking up space on the lot, it'll be yours (and make your offer $150 less this time, just to make a point!).

What they really mean

Cash back offer: Instead of giving you a good price on the car, they inflate the value, and give you some of that money back. Just ask for the best price, without any promotions, and negotiate from there.

No interest: There's no interest until you miss a payment, then they hit you with back interest at loan shark rates.

0% financing: 0% financing ads are always followed by the term OAC – On Approved Credit. Trust me, you won't be approved. But by the time you find this out, you'll have your heart set on the jet black CRV, and won't care if the financing has jumped to 9% or more.

Minimize your car costs

You have to have a car, so you've bought the perfect vehicle. Now you've got to worry about maintenance, insurance, cleaning, parking, gas, and repairs. And you thought buying the car was expensive!

Parking

If you're lucky, parking on campus may be free. On most campuses, though, it isn't free. It's expensive. Parking stalls can run anywhere from $1 to $6 a day, or maybe even more, depending on the lot you choose, or if you have a pass. When Keith worked for Parking Services, he got another perk – a super cheap parking pass for a great lot on campus. It saved us $200 for the year in parking costs. Park in the cheapest lot, or if you're allowed, park near school for free and walk the rest of the way.

Gas

I never used to pay attention to gas prices. I'd just fill up when I needed to, at whatever station was closest. Now I'm a little more careful where I buy gas. Though I refuse to drive across the city for a $0.02 a litre deal,

I will seek out cheap gas and keep an eye out for the better prices. I carry gas cards for all the major retailers – the point cards, not the credit cards. That way, when they offer a few cents off a litre for members, I can take advantage. There might be a chain of stations in your city that consistently offers cheaper gas than anyone else. If so, shop there.

Want to save even more on gas? Use less. When you buy a vehicle, consider the mileage it gets. Keep it running well, with properly inflated tires and regular maintenance. If you can, reduce your use by walking or biking for some errands. Oh, and don't speed or you'll spend more on gas, speeding tickets, and insurance premiums.

Insurance

Shop around for the best insurance rates. While insurance companies, like the banks, are merging and choices are becoming more and more limited, you can still find widely differing quotes when choosing your insurance. Call a few of the companies listed in the yellow pages and get a quote from each. Look for reputable names, and if you get a great rate from a smaller company, check with the Better Business Bureau to ensure they're legitimate.

Ask for a higher deductible. Increasing your deductible from $250 to $500 or even $1,000 can save you hundreds of dollars a year.

Cover only what you need. If you're driving a real beater, comprehensive coverage is probably not required. You'll likely want just the basic coverage.

Buy the right car. Some cars are more expensive to insure, such as sports cars or SUVs. The options or modifications on a vehicle will affect your rates, as well. Buying a car with a booming sub system or one that's lifted six inches will cost you extra. Talk to an insurance company about the cars they red flag.

Ask about discounts. You may be eligible for discounts because of the company you work for or school you attend. If you don't drive often, ask about low mileage discounts. Have a car alarm? It may save you money. If you've never had a claim or ticket, ask for a good driver discount. Driver education grads get a discount, too.

Maintenance

Once you have a car, drive it until it dies. Don't treat it badly – a well-maintained car ensures you spend less on repairs, and you can resell it for more than a beaten up one. But don't buy a new car every year. Once the one you have is paid for, keep it until it conks. When the costs for repairs are looking like they'll be more than the cost of buying a new-to-you car, then it's time to find another ride.

Learn to do regular maintenance yourself. Doing your own oil change can save you $20 each time, which means $80 a year. If you don't already know how, ask your friends and family. Someone will probably be willing to show you. Need new windshield wipers? You can buy the rubber strips separately for half the cost and put them on yourself. Tires worn out? Check used tire stores or discount stores like Wal-Mart for good prices.

Repairs

The key to finding a good repair place that isn't going to rip you off is to ask your friends, colleagues, and co-workers. They'll be able to give you the names of a few places they trust, and you can check them out yourself. Let the manager know you're a student, and he may give you a break. I used to take my car to a shop that would let me buy parts from a used parts place and give them to the repair guy to install. The total cost would be a third of every other price I was quoted.

Do you live in a city with a college or technical school? The automotive repair program might be your ticket. For a small fee, the cost of parts, or sometimes for no charge at all, they will repair bodywork or mechanical problems. The catch is your car might not qualify. They may only need automatics that month, or cars with a certain engine problem. Another downside is they usually need to keep your car a little longer than most other repair shops, and they don't have courtesy cars. But call anyway. Some schools will keep your name on file and will offer to do preventative maintenance.

Roadside assistance

If you're driving an older car, you might want to purchase roadside assistance coverage. It's usually inexpensive, $80 a year or less, and it can pay for itself with one incident. Most major roadside assistance plans cover opening your door if you've locked yourself out of your car, towing service, gas delivery if you run out of gas, battery boosting, and minor emergency repairs. Being a member of a roadside assistance plan may also get you insurance or travel discounts.

Most roadside assistance plans cover you, not your car. This means that if you're out with friends and they need service, you get it for free because you have the plan. This can be handy if you want to help out a friend having car troubles. You could meet and call for assistance then. Your friend gets the free service, you did a good deed, and you got your money's worth out of your membership.

CHAPTER EIGHT
Live Naked

Live Naked is about the necessities of life: health, food, hair, clothes, sex, and other miscellaneous can't-do-withouts.

Don't get sick

Determined to get a summer job as a co-ordinator for the university's new student orientation program, I needed experience participating in the program. So I volunteered as a team leader for the three-day orientation. During training, we were given a tour of the campus, and I discovered an area I had never known existed – the school Health Services office. For years I had been taking an hour-long bus trip to see my doctor, when I could have gone to one on campus! And received free condoms!

Many schools have a health services office complete with nurses, doctors, x-ray machines, etc. They usually offer the same wide array of services a regular medical clinic does, and they sometimes have special services for students, like free doctor's notes for missing exams. And they'll often have free samples of condoms and birth control pills.

We'll fix you – for a fee

Most post-secondary institutions are required to provide medical coverage to their full-time students. If you're still covered by your parents' policy (often full-time students are covered until the age of twenty-five) you can have this coverage waived and your mandatory fee refunded. You may have to submit the paperwork every year, though.

While health care is free in most Canadian provinces, in Alberta, there is a health care premium. It's $44 a month, and separate from the coverage offered by the university. As an Alberta student, you have to pay both. On the plus side, you can get a subsidy for the Alberta Health fee if your income is less than $15,970. If you make less than $12,450, you won't have to pay this fee at all. So if you're tracking your income for the year, and you've got the chance to work a little overtime at Christmas, keep that cost in mind. You might make more money by not working if it bumps your income above subsidy levels.

If you need prescription medication and you don't have coverage, you can try a few tricks. Ask your doctor for samples. They frequently have things like birth control pills they're more than happy to give to you free of charge. When the doctor's writing your prescription, let him know you don't have coverage, and ask for a generic brand if it's available, or the minimum amount of the drug needed. Never try to save money by using leftover, old prescriptions or someone else's medication.

Just like anything else, shop around when filling your prescription. The dispensing fee isn't consistent and can range from $1 to $12, so find the cheapest place before you drop off your prescriptions.

Gerbil it

If you eat right and exercise, sick days should be few and far between. I do cardio exercises three times a week and weights three times a week. While I miss some days, I'm pretty consistent. But I hate working out.

I hate every minute I'm on the Stairmaster or rowing machine. I detest both free weights and weight machines, alike. When I'm running on the treadmill, I'm not getting that mythical runner's high, I'm cursing under my breath. I don't think Nike is going to want my mantra of, "I hate this," for a poster anytime soon. But I do it because every minute I'm not working out, I feel good. Since I began exercising I've become stronger, and I've noticed I fight off colds and flus more easily than ever before. While in school, getting sick hit my wallet hard. Not only did I have to pay for any medications I needed, I also missed a few shifts of work, and part-timers don't get paid sick days.

> **REALITY CHECK:** I have a friend who, before even trying a new sport, outfits himself with the best equipment money can buy. Sometimes he plays the sport just once or twice before deciding it's not his thing, and storing the expensive equipment in the basement. Is he an idiot? Yes. But he can afford to be, and if you can too, you are lucky indeed.

For the rest of us, to participate in sports and keep active for next to nothing takes creativity. You don't need special thermal or wicking technology clothing to run in, just pick up sweats and T-shirts at a thrift store. Buy good sneakers when they're on sale, and keep them just for exercising so you don't wear them out too quickly. Your school probably has a fitness centre, squash courts, a pool, or a skating rink you can use for free – it's usually a mandatory fee. If not, buy used free weights. Your cardio routine requires getting your butt moving, inside or outside. Go for a run or walk, bike, rollerblade, or play a team sport. Whatever it is, just get moving.

Getting laid on a budget

Because Keith and I were together throughout high school and university, I never had to worry about dating on a budget. Anything we did together that might constitute a date (going out for dinner, to movies, etc.) was considered an entertainment expense. I watched friends blow $100 a night for one date, either because they were showing off or they just didn't know how not to go all out. Dinner for two at a nice restaurant can easily cost $100. Add in a movie with a trip to the concession and you're looking at a $150 date. If you can afford that without a second thought, I'm sure I have some single friends I can introduce you to. Seriously though, whether you're trying to impress, or just trying to have a good time, going into debt for dating is ridiculous. Be honest with your dates. Talk about your situation and your goals, and you'll probably find they're in the same situation.

A lot of the ideas for inexpensive entertainment in the next chapter can be used for dates. Looking for a little more romance? Here are a few suggestions:

Take a trip down memory lane. Give your date a tour of your old neighbourhood and home, your elementary school, the convenience store where you used to buy Slurpees and hockey stickers every day. Top off the night by going through old photo albums, and setting a time to do the same for your date.

There's just something about eating a picnic lunch that makes girls swoon. Hike, walk, bike, or drive, and stop for a meal in the wilderness.

Attend free cultural events together (even if you do snicker through them and escape early).

Bike or walk to your nearest ice cream shop. Or go on a hunt to discover the best one in your city. Drive around buying the kids cones at a few places until you've got a headache.

Volunteer together for a clothing drive, at a soup kitchen, or at a work social event.

Spend a few hours playing cards or board games, the ones you loved as a child. There's nothing like a competitive, no-holds-barred game of Risk to discover your date's true personality.

Where you can't cut costs

While the birth control pill is great, and for some monogamous couples it will be the only form of protection they use, if you're not in a committed relationship you always need to use condoms. You know the spiel. The pill doesn't protect you against diseases, and your health and life are worth the money. Buy condoms – they're worth every penny.

Never, ever, buy discount condoms, especially from novelty stores, liquidation stores (yup, I've seen them there) or even out-of-the-way gas stations. You can probably get good quality condoms free from your health services office. Don't be shy; take as many as you can. Replenish your supply often, as condoms do have an expiry date. Don't use them if you think they may have expired, or if they look damaged. Don't carry them around in your wallet, or leave them in your car. When in doubt, throw them out.

I suppose you'll want to eat, too

Food is a big expense, one that will get out of control incredibly easily. You may only stop at the grocery store once every two weeks, and spend less than $40 each time, but that's not your food expense for the month. You've got to count every single food expense, including Slurpee runs, your morning Starbucks fix, the weekly wing night, and Friday dinners out.

Eat more Kraft Dinner

I've always been a frugal shopper when it comes to groceries. Being a Maritimer, I love to splurge on clams, shrimp, scallops, and the occasional lobster. During school, this meant scrimping and saving every possible penny on groceries in order to afford those infrequent luxuries.

The cheapest way to buy groceries is to visit two or three stores for everything you need. If you're bussing it, that's not always possible. But if you can manage it, maybe by getting a ride from a friend, you're better off doing your grocery shopping at a few different locations.

For instance, the produce at my local Co-op is phenomenal. There's tons of variety and it's reasonably priced. Their canned and boxed food however, is usually considerably overpriced compared to the Superstore, which has the best prices for staples like Kraft Dinner and canned soup. When I want meat – chicken, steak, bacon, whatever – I go to Costco. Their prices are much lower than anyone else's for these items, and the quality is good, even for the cheapest cuts of meat.

The danger of Costco is that you leave having bought ten items and spending $300. When I visit, I make a beeline for the meat section, make a quick stop at the bakery, and grab laundry detergent on the way. Before I learned this blinders-on-look-straight-ahead technique, I'd constantly be picking up great books, polar fleece vests, and other gifty types of things for friends, family, and more often than not, myself. And while whatever you buy from Costco will last two years, the huge money hit might blow your food budget out of the water for two months.

Speciality stores

Don't discount speciality stores for great deals on quality food. Though some items might be outside of your budget, you'll often find great deals on the basics. For instance, a tiny Italian supermarket I frequent sells frozen tortellini at half the price of any other grocery stores, even when they have a sale. Check out bakeries for deals on bread or other baked goods, oriental supermarkets for great deals on rice, noodles, and other staples, and Italian stores for sauces or pastas.

Something I always found handy for getting the best prices was to create a shopping guide. I had a list of the thirty items I bought the most, and the usual price I paid. When I saw a lower price, I'd change the price on the list, and would refuse to pay a higher price. When Kraft Dinner was on sale for $0.50 a box instead of the usual $0.89, I'd stock up. I could have bought the no-name brand for $0.50 any day, but with KD, you can tell the difference. Mainly because the wannabe brand tastes like crap. No-name chips, beans, and pasta were fine, but I'm a true Canadian. Mac and cheese has to come from Kraft. It's lame, but eventually you'll have the list memorized.

Freeze it

All through school, I wished I had a freezer. When bread, meat, or ice cream went on sale, I couldn't buy more than one or two portions before the tiny freezer part of the fridge would be packed. I also couldn't cook in bulk. Two casserole dishes were all the freezer could handle. If you're in the same situation, you can still reap the rewards of bulk frozen food purchases if you're imaginative. Find a friend or two in the same predicament and shop together. You can split the packages, and the bill, and still spend less than buying the overpriced goods individually. Beg space in a friend or relative's freezer, or better yet, get your own. You can buy a freezer, new or used, for less than $150 these days. Split the cost with your roommates, or ask for it as a Christmas or birthday gift from your parents.

I get by with a little help from my friends

Justin is a multimedia and design student. He spends just $75 a month on food. "I eat at other people's houses a lot. I'm always willing to give a friend a hand in exchange for pizza and beer, dinner out, etc. Most weekends I eat with family members and the varied menu and richer foods than I normally eat provide a nice change from my daily diet of Kraft Dinner and hot dogs. I never mind when my sister calls for help moving furniture or repainting a room. In return I get to spend time with my family, and get fed!"

Pack it up, pack it in

When I said your food bill includes everything you eat, I meant it. Lunch is a brutal drain on your wallet. You're not at home, the food you did bring looks unappetizing, and your friends are sitting in the food court where all you can smell is greasy, MSG-loaded goodness.

So what do you do? You suck it up, and you pack a lunch. Frozen meals, bought in bulk at a discount food store, cost just $0.99, and cups of soup are even less. Add variety to your packed lunches. Leftovers, frozen dinners, canned soup, and sandwiches are all traditional lunch fare, but no one ever said you couldn't have a little fun. Real cheese and crackers, fresh fruit salad, frozen juice boxes, and other unique fare will keep you from buying a lunch out of boredom. To ensure your food doesn't get smashed, use empty margarine containers to pack fruit and other delicate items.

But keep in mind that while packing a lunch is cheap, buying a lunch can sometimes be cheaper. I lived off the $2 rice and dumpling deal on campus for a whole year, switching to the $1.29 salads on days when I had less change. On days when I was working downtown, where the pop was $2, I packed my lunch. I made creative, delicious meals for less than $2. Compared to the $7 "value" burger deals at fast food joints, bringing a lunch from home or sourcing out the cheapest food deals around will allow you to spend much less.

Learn to cook

Convenience food will be the death of you, financially and nutritionally. I'm the first to admit that my weakness for Coca-Cola is chewing holes through my wallet, and probably my stomach lining. So skip the pre-packaged junk and dig out your apron, it's time you learned to cook.

They say necessity is the mother of all invention, and in my case it was certainly true. I became interested in cooking because I had to. When my parents divorced, my mom started working full-time, taking the bus to and from work. She got home late, after 6:30 p.m. most nights. If we wanted to eat a normal family dinner together, I'd have to cook it, or else we'd be eating at 7:30 p.m. I started out small – Rice-A-Roni was a common side dish and Shake'n Bake-something usually the main course. I still recall burning every single cookie in a batch of five dozen. Each time the oven temperature light went out I'd turn up the heat, thinking the oven was turning off. I had no idea what pre-heating was, and my mother nearly killed herself laughing when she found me trying to bake cookies in a 550°F oven.

Eventually I gained some skill, and moved on to more complex dishes. I watch the Food Network, and can recreate many gourmet dishes in my own kitchen. Still, our family favourite and three-meals-a-week special is mushroom noodles (a can of mushroom soup, a little milk, and egg noodles.). It's quick, and half the cost of buying a frozen pasta entree.

Preparing your own food from the basic ingredients (I don't say "scratch," as that connotes grinding wheat into flour and crushing tomatoes by hand) is a great way to stretch your food dollar. With a can of tomato sauce, dry pasta, a few spices, and cream cheese, you can make a fresh, creamy, rich dinner, with plenty of leftovers, for just a few dollars.

If you're hopeless in the kitchen, borrow a few cookbooks from friends or family. You'll easily find people willing to lend or even give you their cookbooks. Most households have a few that have never been used. Read the front and back pages for tips and tricks on how to understand the recipes. Find cookbooks written for students or young people, and books that tout their recipes as easy, fast, or inexpensive.

Have you ever used a Crock-Pot? This throwback from the '80s is a busy person's saving grace. Throw meat, veggies, a little seasoning, and sauce in the pot in the morning and by the time you get home you'll have a delicious meal waiting to be eaten in front of the TV. Just don't forget to turn it on, or you'll have a cold, congealed pot of nastiness. Most people have a Crock-Pot, and if they're not using it, ask if they'll lend it to you, or try to find one at a yard sale or thrift store.

Perfect recipes online

I love the experience of buying or receiving a new cookbook, reading the recipes, visualizing the dinner party I'll serve them at, and savouring over the descriptions. While I'll never stop loving the traditional cookbook, the Internet has changed the way I cook. Web sites like www.allrecipes.com list thousands of recipes. The site is attractively designed, easy to navigate, and best of all, it's free. You can search by recipe name or ingredient, or browse by type of food. Each recipe has a spot where you can read or post reviews, some of which will have suggestions for easier preparation or substitutions. I seek out highly rated recipes, and after making dozens, from entrees to cakes, I've never had a bad experience.

Gourmet or novice, you'll need a few basics, like spices, condiments, flour, and sugar. You'll need to buy certain items as soon as you move out on your own, and infrequently after that. Buying spices is a killer. Check out spice racks that come equipped with a supply of basic spices. While spices lose their flavour after a few months, they're still good, just not quite as potent. Use more in your recipes, or buy fresh spices and split the bag with a friend.

The food plan scam

I know, I've already complained about this. Food plans for rez students are a huge rip-off. The basic plan is more expensive than buying your own food and eating like a king! I recommend you buy the cheapest plan and supplement your menu at your local grocery store. If you find you're spending more using this method than you would on a more expensive plan, make the switch. Most schools will allow you to increase your plan without charging an administration fee, but they will charge the fee if you choose to decrease your plan.

Don't think your rez food plan is reasonably priced? Let the university know. As my monthly food plan shows, eating balanced, nutritious, and appetizing meals on a limited budget is possible. If enough students complain, the school will listen. Maybe they need to look at scaling back the variety of choices to reduce costs, preparing more basic dishes. You could scout out good restaurant deals and eat for less than $10 a day. Why not demand the same service of the food plan? Or fight for the option of choosing not to buy into the food plan. Giving students a choice would put the responsibility for providing good quality and reasonably priced products back on the shoulders of the food services department.

Food banks and you

Most schools have a student food bank. We never had to use it, but we came pretty close a few times. Many students would prefer to put their groceries on their Visa and let the balance ride than try the food bank, but if you qualify, you might as well use this service. It's confidential, and the people are friendly and professional. Each food bank has different guidelines, but you usually get a food basket that will contain one or two weeks' worth of groceries, and you can visit the food bank only once during a set number of weeks. Don't be a martyr – go there if you need to. When you move up in the world, be sure to make a donation.

Bad hair days

Over the years, I've tried many different hair salons. My hair has been massacred by a $130-an-hour hack in an upscale salon, and perfectly coifed by the chain-smoking senior at a $10 chop shop. As with many things, sometimes paying more for a service doesn't mean you're getting better quality.

If you're looking to spend as little as possible on your hair, you've got a few options. When my husband tired of spending $30 and an hour in a salon for a five-minute cut, I bought a hair trimmer set. For the price of one haircut, I've been cutting his hair for more than a year. It looks just as good, and we can do it in less than ten minutes whenever he needs a trim.

If cutting your own hair isn't an option, try your local Supercuts, MasterCuts, or another hairdressing chain. Their prices are quite reasonable, and if you have a low-maintenance hairstyle, their work is fine. If you'd like something a little more upscale but still don't want to blow all your hard-earned cash, try a beauty school. Students work out of the school's salon to gain experience, and charge much lower rates than other salons. The work is supervised and usually just as good as any other salon. A lot of people have caught onto this deal, so you might need to book a few weeks in advance.

Hair care isn't just about haircuts. To pull off a good look, you have to have product. Salons, commercials, and even friends will try to talk you into buying incredibly overpriced jars of hair care product, but I encourage you to be more resourceful. While some products really are superior to the no-name brands, most are just hype.

Case in point. As a teenager, Keith worked in a factory where they made two brands of a certain food product. In the morning they'd fill bags of the no-name, inexpensive product as it poured through the chutes. In the afternoon they bagged the expensive stuff. One day they needed more of the expensive product, and mid-way through the morning shift the supervisor asked the guys to change the bags. Keith prepared to take a break, but an older guy stopped him. Keith had assumed other workers would clean out the machine and put in the better product, something he figured was done while he was on lunch each day. This wasn't the case. Instead of changing the product, they just changed the bag.

I've retold this story many times, and over the years I've learned of a few other companies that do this. While some companies will alter something minor in the product to differentiate it, like the colour or scent, many companies don't even bother doing that. They think we won't know the difference. And we don't.

Buy your hair care products from the grocery store or local drug-store. If you think there really is a difference, buy product only when it's on sale, and buy in bulk. Use your network. If you have a friend or relative in hairdressing, ask if they can buy you product at cost. Look for sales, but don't use them as an excuse to buy stuff you don't need.

Bonne Bell vs. MAC – can money buy beauty?

You are not going to be more gorgeous because you wear more expensive makeup. In fact, in her best-selling cosmetics bible, *Don't Go to the Cosmetics Counter Without Me*, author Paula Begoun examines more than two hundred brands and thousands of products, from moisturizers to mascara, and rates them based on their ingredients and effectiveness. She identifies the good buys, inexpensive substitutes, and misleading claims. Borrow this book from your local library and read what she says about the top brands. You'll be amazed. Armed with Paula's knowledge, you'll feel confident buying the inexpensive items that you truly need without buying into the pretty packaging.

Thrift shops – beyond the Seattle grunge look

Remember Adbusters? As part of their creative resistance efforts they've designed a number of spoof ads highlighting how ridiculous and even dangerous many of the products we use every day really are. Here's my personal favourite, a spoof ad for Tommy Hilfiger.

You can go to school in your pyjamas. In fact, on any campus that's how you pick out the frosh – they dress well. During school nobody really cares what you wear, but you can't go to work dressed like a bum. So if you're going to justify spending money on clothes, they better be "work clothes" – they're the only kind worth buying for the next few years.

Buying clothes at regular prices from a high-end store is your absolute last resort. There are so many other, less expensive ways of getting decent clothing that it's an unnecessary waste, and a frivolous thing to put you into debt.

Trade

Instead of dropping your own clothes off at a clothing bin, share your clothes with friends. Okay, I really can't picture guys spending an afternoon trading their old clothes and catching up, so this is probably only a good tip for women. Talk to your girlfriends about saving unwanted clothing and having a trade day. Everyone can bring in their clothes, spend an afternoon trying things on, and take home bags full of "new to you" stuff.

If your friends, or you, aren't interested in a trade day, take your unwanted clothing to a consignment shop that lets you sell your clothes. These shops will take a percentage of the money when the item sells. Keep an eye on the calendar, as most shops will keep the full amount if you don't return within a year to claim your money or your clothes.

A quick way to update your wardrobe is to trade with friends, but not for keeps. Whether you're borrowing a great jacket for a party or a skirt for work, swapping clothes for awhile lets you feel like you've got something new, but before you get tired of it you get to give it back. Take good care of the item, return it clean, and be willing to lend the friend an item in exchange. Because you never know what can happen, be willing to lose it, too. Don't lend anyone the sweater your late grandma knitted.

Thrift stores

Buy clothes at thrift stores. Sometimes you can find really interesting items in good shape. I remember the first time I went into a thrift shop. I found a great sweater for $5, but it was a little worn. I didn't buy it, and bought a similar one brand new for $40 instead. Three weeks later, after I had washed the new sweater just three times, it was already look-ing a little stretched and worn. I could have just bought the used one! Five years later, I still have the sweater. Wish I had the $35.

The girls in my office are from all walks of life, but one thing we have in common is the thrill of the hunt. Every so often we'll pile into someone's car at lunch and hit Value Village, a huge thrift store. We don't just look for ourselves, but for each other. Anything cool is grabbed. If it's not your size, someone else might fit it and like it. Value Village shopping is a team effort for us, and taking home three or four good "work clothes" sweaters for $10 is a very productive lunch.

If cruising the aisles of your local Sally Ann doesn't do it for you, you can find the better second-hand clothing stores in nicer neighbourhoods.

Check your local yellow pages under consignment. The prices are steeper than a charity-run thrift store, but they have better clothes. If you shop at the same one you sell your clothes at, you can take credit, and some stores give you more value in credit than they do in cash.

Brand spankin' new

So, you have to have new stuff. For underwear, socks, T-shirts, sweats, and any trendy item that won't last more than a season, shop at Wal-Mart, Zellers, or another cheap place.

If you want better stuff with labels, wait until you graduate. Remember, buy Good Enough for Now! Okay, I know you sometimes won't, so when shopping for good gear, hit the malls in late January and February. The stores are so desperate for shoppers after everyone has drained their wallets over the holidays they usually have major clearance sales on. Ask for gift certificates for your favourite clothing stores for Christmas and use them during the sales.

Buy things with staying power. Plain jeans without trendy effects like rips or fringes will carry your wardrobe longer than the pair with imitation dirt stains. Not only will the trendy jeans look dated before you wear them out, but it will also be easier to tell that you've worn them twice in a week.

Keep in mind though, staying power isn't the same as buying something the salesperson claims is "timeless." I recently saw a poster at a clothing store showing ten items that could be co-ordinated into twenty-five outfits, or something ridiculous like that. They were "classic" and "timeless" pieces that would be in style for years. While I applaud the idea of buying clothes that you can mix and match to minimize your clothing costs, I don't think any clothes are timeless. A few years after purchase, the fabric isn't cut quite right, the colour is a little off, the hem is too long, the waist is too high. This can happen even with something as simple as a plain white shirt. The cuff size, button placement, and collar length will date the item, probably long before you wear it out. So don't be talked into buying an $80 sweater because it will be a timeless piece. It may be a good quality garment that will last forever, but you won't care that it still fits when you suddenly think it's ugly as hell. And yes, retro is cool, but it has to be at least ten years old to come back in style.

Add items to your wardrobe only if they fit with whatever you already have. I used to make the mistake of buying a great skirt only to find I had no shoes that matched. The $10 skirt was a deal, but the $45 shoes to match weren't. I do have a fabulous pair of chunky snakeskin boots that get worn twice a year, but for $9.99 on clearance, they're my one irrational shoe purchase. If you find a killer pair of shoes that you know you'll only wear occasionally, feel free to buy them – if they're $9.99. Just don't do it every weekend.

If you're looking for clothing for a special event, but a one-time-use suit doesn't fit in your budget, consider buying an item, wearing it once, and returning it the next day. I know, I'm evil, very bad, should never have suggested it. While most stores frown on this, lots of people do it, and I've even had store associates suggest that when I mentioned I couldn't afford an item but really needed it. Keep the tags on, and don't spill anything, or you'll be adding the item to your wardrobe permanently.

Pink leather jacket

It started with a simple flyer in the mail. Danier Leather was having a fall sale, and a suede jacket I had been eyeing was just $99. Armed with the flyer, a hundred bucks, and determination, I visited the store. An hour later I walked out with the suede jacket – and a pink leather one.

I don't know what I was thinking. The mirrors in the store were slimming, the lights flattering to all colours. But I didn't own a single other article of pink clothing. And it really was pink. A cotton candy, Pepto-Bismol kind of pink.

I was thinking of swallowing my pride and returning it when the worst thing that could have happened did – Keith saw the jacket. As expected, he exploded. He ranted about the cost, how ugly it was, and my inability to maintain any self-control around leather. I found myself fighting back, defending the hideous pink jacket.

As much as I swore I loved the jacket and would wear it everywhere, I never did. After a year, I couldn't bear having this garish reminder of my mistake rustling in the back of the closet and gave it to a colleague who loved it. To this day, my husband cannot let an opportunity pass by without mentioning the pink leather jacket. Friends and family kindly bring it up occasionally. In fact, when I told a few people the idea for this book, they helpfully suggested including a tip about not buying pink leather jackets. It's nice to have such supportive friends.

The pink leather jacket incident taught me to never buy anything on impulse. Admire it, try it on, and put it back on the rack. If you still want the item in two weeks and you absolutely can afford it without going into debt or sacrificing something more important, go back and look at it again. If it's gone, it wasn't meant to be. If it's still there, buy it. Unless it's a pink leather jacket.

Always keep your receipts

Have you ever bought an item only to find it on sale a week later? If you keep the receipt, you can get what's called a price adjustment. The store will give you back the difference between what you paid for the item and the sale price. Some stores will make price adjustments up to six months after your purchase. For big-ticket items, it pays to check the price again later. Some stores will even give you a sale price before a sale starts – the Bay and Sears are great for this.

Don't throw out a clothes receipt until a year after purchase. Many stores have a No Sale is Ever Final policy. They'll accept clothes back for an exchange or refund months after your purchase if you decide you don't like it after wearing it once, if a seam tears in the wash, or if a button falls off.

Laundry day

Once we moved out, our basement suite didn't have a washer or dryer. We washed as much as we could in the kitchen sink, hung everything to dry, and reused towels (you're supposed to be clean when you're using them, right?). Anything that had to be cleaned in a washing machine was hauled to mom's house, or in a pinch, done at the local laundromat. "Dry clean only" was not in our vocabulary.

As I usually worked in an office, I've always had two wardrobes, even when I worked in casual environments. Even today I treat my office clothes with better care – I change the minute I walk in the door and hang still-clean items up immediately. My non-office wardrobe was extremely limited during school, but like my mom used to say when I was in junior high and wanted to get all tarted up, "You're not going to a fashion show."

To save money, and wear and tear on your clothes, change the moment you get home. Don't wear your Friday office jeans to the bar on the weekend or your dress shirts around the house all night. By removing and hanging clothes as soon as you get home they'll need to be washed less, and you'll have less of an opportunity to accidentally spill something on them.

If you have friends or family members with washers and dryers, ask if you can use them. Most laundromats change $3 to $5 for a tiny load of laundry. You could offer the friend $1 or $2 for each load you do. If you must go to a laundromat, go to one in a lower rent area of town to get cheaper rates, and always bring your own detergent.

One more thing

Buy only the bare necessities – the minimum amount of clothing, hair care products, or makeup. Being a clotheshorse doesn't make you a better person, it doesn't get you better grades, and it certainly doesn't make you more money. Figure out where you can cut costs on these necessities to ensure you keep working step by step towards your goal.

CHAPTER NINE
You're a Student, You Don't Get a Life

Whether you party every weekend or only go out to celebrate special events, having fun and spending money seem synonymous. That was old you. Debt-free you knows the hangover from a wild and expensive night will have you praying to the porcelain god and wondering where your rent money went. This chapter is full of ideas for finding and enjoying inexpensive or free entertainment. Grab your daytimer (the one you got from school for free) and read on.

Your bedroom, your entertainment complex

Cable TV may just be your biggest entertainment expense. Most nights you can find a show or two to watch instead of going to a movie or going out to the bar. If you're busy a few nights in a row, tape your favourite shows to watch when you have more time. Tape a few weeks of shows and have a personal television marathon. The hit television show, "Survivor," started a "Survivor night" phenomenon where people would gather at bars, pubs, and in each other's homes just to watch the show. You can do the same with "The Sopranos," "America's Funniest Home Videos," or "Boston Public." Whatever it is, congregate at a friend's place, pitching in for beverages and snacks.

Instead of going to a movie theatre, rent flicks and watch them from the comfort of your home. The seating is more comfortable, the food cheaper and better, and you can pause for a bathroom break. Why do we even go to the theatre anymore? The thrill of watching a movie on the big screen fades quickly when you realize you've spent ten times what it would have cost you to rent a video, and buy hot air popcorn and a two-litre bottle of pop.

Most video stores have discount nights, so be sure to stop by then. If your local store has a Guaranteed New Release policy, make sure you ask if they have a copy of the film you want. If they don't have any at all, they have to give you a coupon to rent it free next time. If you have friends who go to the real theatres, ask if you can have their ticket stubs. It can get you free or discounted movies at the video store.

Chances are, one of your friends is a movie freak. Lucky for me, many of my friends are addicted to building their DVD collections. Heading into the weekend I simply stop by their house to see what new movies they've got, and grab a few. If you borrow frequently from many friends, keep a sticky note on the case to ensure you get the right movie back to the right person.

Clip coupons

For your next birthday, ask for an Entertainment book, Student Union Ticket Pack, or whatever other entertainment savings book your city has to offer. You'll find coupons for most attractions in your city, as well as deals on restaurants and services. In many cities the Entertainment book has $60 worth of $5 coupons for grocery stores – that alone makes purchasing the $40 book a good deal. Receive the book as a gift and you'll be set.

You don't need a dorky flowered coupon book to keep your coupons in, either. Scrounge up a big bulletin board and pin them up where you can see them. Keep ones you may use on the fly in your wallet for easy access.

Once you start looking, you'll be surprised how many coupons you come across every day. The junk mail flyers you usually trash? The newspaper left out on a desk? Even your phone bill may come with coupons.

You can find coupons online at Web sites like www.save.ca, where you simply choose your province, then select the coupons or samples you want to have mailed to you. At www.coupons.com you can also view coupons based on your location, but you'll have to print them yourself.

Movies

- Ignore the megascreen movie complexes. They charge inflated admission prices, sell you $1.10 worth of pop and popcorn for $11, show commercials before the movie, and have the thermostat set at permafrost. To catch a new flick, hit the second-run theatres, and motor right past the concession.
- If you don't mind a little spam, sign up for the online newsletter at your local video store. Rogers Video sends e-mails with a coupon for a free new release or seven-day rental. No strings attached!
- Do you work for a company with a lot of young people? Call the major entertainment studios' promotions departments and ask for free passes to new screenings for your co-workers. During the winter months, when attendance wanes, sales reps will send screening passes to anyone who requests them, just to encourage word-of-mouth buzz on a flick.
- Just like music, you can download movies on your computer at home for free. Always be careful when using your computer to download fun stuff. It won't be nearly as fun when you get hit with a virus and have to buy a new hard drive.

Sports

- Get some school pride. Most sports events held by your school are free for students to attend.
- Ask about student rates for tickets for local sports teams.
- Want to get into the game? Instead of playing for a formal league, find people interested in pick-up games, or join an intramural league. If you're a star player, the quality of the games might not be the level you're accustomed to, but the

price is right, usually free or a few bucks a game.

- Some sports can be expensive. Limit your participation, and spend only the absolute minimum required. Heading to the hills for a day of snowboarding? Carpool, go on student days, borrow the equipment, and pack a lunch.

Bars

- Don't go – drink at home.
- You're determined to go to the bar and get hammered. Make the night cheaper by drinking at home before hitting the bar, but be sure to have a designated driver.
- If you don't mind getting to a club before it's jumping, you'll avoid the line, the cover, and probably score free drink tickets.
- Drink on student night, or ask for student prices.
- Find out the specials, then drink those.
- If you're not drinking alcohol, talk to a bartender about free pop. Most bars offer it when asked. If not, bring or buy a water bottle and refill it at the tap.
- Always have a reliable designated driver. A taxi ride to the 'burbs will blow your entertainment money for the month.
- Bring a flask – just don't get busted with it.
- If your shot costs more than $4, you bought the glass. Stick it in your purse or cargo pants pocket and add it to your home collection.

Alcohol

- Keep an eye on flyers for sales, and for price comparisons.
- Bigger liquor stores often have free memberships that get you great prices. Become a member if you shop there often.
- When you find a great price, buy in bulk.
- Taste test the no-name brands, and buy those instead of paying for an advertising budget. If the price is right, buy the product that gives you free stuff – glasses, shirts, and caps are the usual freebies.
- While big box stores like Safeway or Superstore liquor stores

usually have the best average prices, smaller stores often sell certain products at unbeatable prices to encourage traffic. Keep an eye out for neon signs touting great deals.

- If you drink a lot, think about making your own beer or wine. It may not taste as good, but it'll do the trick!

Dining out

- Go during the week. Many restaurants have special prices Monday to Wednesday evenings.
- Drink water, not beer or pop. The mark-up on these items is high, and you don't get much value for your money.
- Try something new. Look for restaurants that have buy-one-get-one-free entree offers in your coupon books. It's a chance to try new restaurants and eat well for less.
- Instead of going out for dinner, just go out for dessert and coffee. You'll still have the experience of going out at half the cost.
- Don't forget to tip. If you get phenomenal service but can't afford to give a tip better than the minimum 10%, write a note to the manager before you leave. Your server will appreciate the gesture.
- Instead or ordering two entrees, order one large entree and a side item. Ask for an extra plate and split the two dishes.
- Skip dessert. If you have a craving for something sweet, stop at an ice cream place on your way home or pick up a small tub of expensive ice cream. You'll have a delicious treat and keep more money in your pocket.

Get paid to shop!

Have you ever heard the term "mystery shopper"? Also known as secret shoppers, they are regular people who are paid to shop. Mystery shoppers are given "shops" or "assignments" and receive detailed instructions, which may include how much to spend, when to shop, and even what scenarios to act out. The mystery shopper must complete the shop, mentally recording a variety of details, including employee names, conversations, store cleanliness, and employee interactions with other customers. After the shop, the mystery shopper completes an evaluation form, giving an objective account of what happened during the shop. For most mystery shopping companies, the logistics of this process are available online, from the choice of shops to the evaluation forms, and even payment requests.

While mystery shopping isn't going to make you rich, it is a fun and interesting way to earn a little extra cash. Some companies offer a flat fee for completing the shop, while others offer a flat fee as well as credit towards a purchase. You can choose from a variety of assignments, from retail shops to restaurant and hotel visits. You can get your oil changed, have a gourmet dinner, or get a new pair of sneakers – all for free!

Depending on the mystery shopping company, you can expect to work according to your availability and interest. Some shoppers complete just one or two shops per month, while others can do twenty or more. If you're interested in becoming a mystery shopper, you'll need your own transportation and Internet access. When signing up with a company as a shopper, be careful. Some Web sites have been promoting get rich quick scams through mystery shopping. These sites sell mystery shopping company lists, and make unrealistic claims about shoppers receiving free trips or vehicles. Avoid these scams, and do your own searching online or follow the links provided below. Registration is always free with reputable mystery shopping companies.

http://www.sqm.ca
http://www.acnielsen.com
http://www.checkmarkinc.com/
http://www.shopnchek.com/
http://www.thecrg.com/
http://www.rapidchek.com/

The beat goes on

The advent of Napster and other music file-sharing programs changed the face of music. Instead of shelling out $20 or more for a CD with just one or two good songs, you could download music off the Internet for free, creating your own personalized collections. You could even get songs before they were released, and burn your own CDs.

The downside is it's stealing. Well, at least some people think so. Personally, I'm looking at my collection of more than four hundred CDs and thinking, "There are probably less than 1,000 good songs on all those CDs, and I paid more than $6,000 for them." So while I recognize downloading is technically stealing, I think the industry needed a wake-up call about the price of music. Besides, Napster and the other music file-sharing programs have not significantly impacted the profits of the recording industry. Sometimes you just want the CD. Do I feel sorry for the overpaid, under-worked, mega-artists? No. But I do feel sorry for the little guys, especially Canadian bands, so when I have the cash I buy their CD instead of downloading the music.

But you're a student, and buying CDs is an unnecessary expense at this point in your life. Napster may be gone, but there are plenty of file-sharing programs still out there. Download your music, or borrow from friends or the library. Better yet, listen to the radio.

The worst part of enjoying music isn't the price of CDs, it's the price of concerts, which are being priced right out of anyone's budgets. $50 to see U2 or the Rolling Stones, rock legends both, used to seem like a lot of money. Now they command $200 a ticket. In protest of incredibly high prices, I refuse to go to concerts anymore. It's not just the artists who charge a bundle for concerts, either. TicketMaster, with its ticket monopoly, charges as much as $10 or more in service fees per ticket. Fill a stadium and they're raking in hundreds of thousands of dollars in revenue, just for selling the tickets. And the worst part is, it's not going to get better. TicketMaster has been losing money for years, so they're not likely to lower the service charges anytime soon.

If you're seriously into concerts and really want to see them, you may not have to pay for them.

Volunteer as an usher, security guard, or general event worker.

If you're a concert reviewer for a student paper, community weekly, or online zine, you'll usually get passes to concerts for free. I saw Our Lady Peace and Céline Dion that way. Though as you can see from my example, the downside is you can't always be picky about what you see.

Try to win tickets through radio contests.

Join a fan club. Some bands do free shows just for their fan club members, so check out your favourite band's Web site to see if they offer something similar.

Promote your favourite group. They may offer free tickets if you help promote the show in your area by putting up posters, giving out flyers, etc.

Saving money on concert tickets can be as simple as changing your listening habits. Attend concerts at smaller venues by local or indie bands. I remember seeing Great Big Sea for $8 at the university just after their first album was released. Now they charge $50 or more. We did pay $45 once for a Great Big Sea concert, which didn't live up to the experience of that first $8 show. You can always find a $5 to $10 concert somewhere. Your community or campus weekly should have listings.

Campus fun

Right on campus you'll find loads of inexpensive entertainment ideas. Pick up your student newspaper for listings of plays, recitals, art shows, athletic events, special lectures, or readings. Join a club – you'll get discounts for events or retailers selling related products and meet new people with similar interests. Being a club member looks good on scholarship and job applications, too.

Campus clubs often host free events for members and non-members alike, including:

- Career networking events
- Cheesy movie nights
- Guest speakers (with free munchies)

Cheap and creative

You're working part-time, attending classes full-time, studying, researching, exercising, grocery shopping, and applying for scholarships – and you still have free time? Here are some cheap entertainment ideas:

- Walk through a local park, stopping for ice cream cones.
- Get active. Spend an afternoon rollerblading, biking, walking, or hiking.
- Attend a play on student night, or Pay What You Can performances. If you live in Calgary or Ottawa, check out www.liverush.ca for information on last-minute student deals on great seats at top art performances.
- Dust off the Monopoly board. Invite friends over to play cards, dominoes, or board games.
- Check out amateur night at your local... comedy club. What did you think I was going to say?
- Instead of girls' night out at the bar, host a sleepover. Pop popcorn, watch a chick flick, and reconnect with your girlfriends.
- Most museums have a free admission day. Pack a lunch and avoid the gift shop.
- There's nothing more fun than acting like a kid again. Find toboggans or Krazy Karpets for cheap in the spring, and after heavy snowfalls the following winter grab your friends for a few hours on the hills.
- Go stargazing. Bring a children's astronomy book from the library.
- No one to play Scrabble with? Join a gaming room on the Internet. Find your favourite game and challenge people around the world.
- Go skating at an outdoor rink.
- Pack a picnic and visit a local lake, or take a drive in the country.
- Think like a tourist. Go for a stroll in the city's shopping districts, window shopping only.
- Round up friends for a game of touch football in a local park.

Sign me up!

I admit it – I'm a loyalty card junkie. I hunt for opportunities to rack up my points. I love the rush of proudly hauling out the appropriate chunk of plastic, in gold. New acquaintances invariably scoff at my collection. "You never earn enough points for anything," they mock. "You pay more in interest than the rewards are worth," they laugh.

So I tell them about my spaghetti sauce revelation.

Safeway was offering bonus Air Miles when you purchased twenty cans of spaghetti sauce. For a $20 investment in spaghetti sauce, I received three hundred Air Miles. For a return trip from Calgary to Moncton in off-peak season, I needed 2,800 Air Miles. Using the spaghetti can system, the ticket cost me less than $200! If you're living away from home and facing a big bill to go back in the summer, being a savvy Air Miles collector could get you there for very little money.

So they're not having a spaghetti deal anytime soon. You can still collect Air Miles and rack them up quickly. Most weeks the local newspaper prints bonus Air Miles coupons. By spending $100, I received an additional one hundred Air Miles. By spending $300 on groceries a month, I can earn three hundred extra Air Miles.

What can you do with just a hundred and fifty Air Miles? More than you'd think. You can redeem them for a free Famous Players Night Out pass. The pass includes two adult admissions, two pops, and one popcorn. In Calgary, that's a $40 value per pass! You can also redeem Air Miles for sports tickets, theatre tickets, and merchandise. The Air Miles program is an exceptional one, especially since it's free. But there are other programs out there that can also give you the rewards you want, for little investment.

Take credit cards. Many offer point programs redeemable for travel, merchandise, or savings on purchases. After much research I chose the Visa Classic Two card. For an annual fee of just $15 (free when I was a student), this card gives me one point for every dollar spent. Spend $2,500 and you receive a Famous Players Night Out pass. I'm careful to put all my purchases on my Visa to get the points, and just as careful to pay the balance each and every month.

Some loyalty card programs just aren't worth the hassle. I've actually been offered cards that cost more to sign up for than it was possible to earn in rewards! For instance, a bookstore I frequent offers a card for under $30, and gives you a portion of your purchases back. The catch? The card is only good for the year, and you have to spend many hundreds of dollars to get a few bucks back. Shop at a used bookstore instead!

Tips

Store loyalty cards: Don't spend $100 at Store A to get a $5 reward, when the same item at Store B costs $80 with no reward.

Prepare for junk mail! It's the downside of being a loyalty cardholder.

Credit card programs: Be careful! Rewards aren't worth it if you carry a large balance and pay interest. Get a card with a point program and a low interest rate. Also, if you sign up for a card just to get the free shirt, gift certificate, or other gift with approval, you could mess up your credit by having so many credit checks on your file.

Don't pay for loyalty cards unless you're sure you'll spend enough at the store to get a return on the investment.

Read the fine print, look for the deals, and know when to jump on the points train.

Online programs

As if you don't get enough junk e-mail, there's an online points program called MyPoints that rewards you just for reading messages.

Once you sign up for the program at www.mypoints.com you'll begin to receive e-mails, a few per week, with offers to purchase items online or try something free, like a magazine subscription.

While the deals may be tempting, you don't have to buy anything to collect points. You simply click on the "Visit Web site" link provided in the e-mail. To collect points faster you can purchase items featured in the e-mails, but that's defeating the purpose, isn't it?

It takes reading a lot of e-mails to earn the points required for a reward, but once or twice a year you'll receive gift certificates for a Canadian store of your choice, including Blockbuster, Roots, or the Olive Garden. All it takes is a lot of clicks and a little bit of willpower.

Dance, baby, dance!

I love to dance. My absolute favourite thing to do on a Saturday night is to go dancing. Usually a night at the bar can cost an arm and a leg, but I've got it down to a $10 adventure. First I grab my younger brother, who also happens to love dancing. For $2 we can park a block from the club. Our favourite bar has a five bucks, five drinks promotion Saturday nights if you arrive before 10:30 p.m. The bar's a little dead at that time, but it gives Justin and me a chance to talk and catch up. Since I know I'll be driving, and I don't drink much anyway, I use one drink ticket and give Justin the rest. When I'm done the first drink, I find a friendly-looking bartender and ask for a Coke. I ask, "I'm driving tonight, can I get free refills if I come back to you?" They always say yes. I tip $3 for the first drink, and try not to let the busboy steal my glass. By 11:00 p.m. the dance floor is respectably full, and I get out there. A few hours later I drop Justin off at home. I'm home by 1:30 a.m., just $10 lighter.

The local library and you

So you're not a reader? Why not become one? The library is a great free entertainment resource. From novels and CDs to cookbooks and magazines, your local library has it all. Many libraries now allow you to review catalogues, reserve, and renew books online. You can also take out copies of magazines, or sit and read current ones. The daily paper's available, as is an Internet connection if you don't have it at home.

If you want a specific book or magazine your library doesn't have, ask if they'll purchase it. They frequently add specific titles to their collection upon request.

Volunteer with ulterior motives

There are more than 6.5 million volunteers in Canada. Volunteering has many benefits, some of which are a little selfish. I know, you volunteer because you're a good person and expect nothing in return but that warm fuzzy feeling you get from doing something good. But volunteering can also help you make contacts in your field, gain marketable skills, and look good on scholarship and job applications. If you're working part-time and going to school full-time, finding time to volunteer is a nearly impossible task, but you don't need to save the world. Even two or three hours a week could be useful to some organizations.

You can find interesting and rewarding volunteer opportunities in your local newspaper, on school bulletin boards, or just by calling not-for-profit organizations you're interested in. And volunteering doesn't mean you'll be stuffing envelopes or cleaning animal cages. You can target your good deeds to your area of expertise or an area that needs improvement. If you need to gain office experience, ask to help type minutes, file, or mail newsletters. Ask to write the newsletter! Want to build a Web design portfolio? Create a Web site at no charge for a local not-for-profit. A cosmetology student can give time at a senior's residence to provide services for the elderly, while someone interested in construction can contact Habitat for Humanity to see where they can help. Whatever your interest, I'm certain there's an opportunity for you to volunteer and reap the benefits, both material and spiritual.

Not sure you'll find a volunteer position that's right for you, and your resumé? There are plenty of organizations out there that are very aware you're not just in it for the sake of your soul. Take Meal Exchange for example. At seventeen, Rahul Raj was a first-year student at Wilfrid Laurier University. He founded Meal Exchange, a charitable organization designed to "promote student civic engagement through the development of solutions to hunger." Their programs are simple. "Skip a Meal" asks students with meal plans to donate unused points to Meal Exchange to purchase products most needed by local food banks and social service agencies. "Trick or Eat" has costumed students canvass their neighbourhoods on Halloween collecting canned goods instead of candy for the local hungry. "Clear the Shelves!" allows students to donate unused food at the end of the academic year instead of lugging it home for the summer. Meal Exchange chapters exist at forty-five post-secondary institutions across Canada and participants would like to see it expanded to every educational institution.

Meal Exchange is a great example of how you can find many different volunteer roles within one organization. They also provide volunteers with the support of board members for mentoring and guidance. Here's their list of volunteer jobs:

Web site development: Refine the presentation of our existing Web site and prepare for v.4.0. of www.mealexchange.com.

Technology solutions: Identify and implement technology-based solutions to facilitate program delivery, i.e. online video conferencing.

Public relations: Promotion of Meal Exchange's Web site and online hunger forum amongst students, professors, and social service stakeholders.

Event planning: Plan and manage a signature Meal Exchange event.

Food service negotiation: Maximize student donations by leading negotiations with the Big 3 food service management teams.

Performance tracking: Identify the optimal tracking measures and tools for Meal Exchange programs.

Volunteer management: Develop and test a volunteer model to optimize a student's volunteer experience and foster a sense of community.

Revenue generation: Secure funds through traditional vehicles and aid the organization in developing a sustainable revenue model to facilitate self-sufficiency.

Brand management: Identify, evaluate, and manage opportunities for advertising, marketing, and promotion of Meal Exchange and its programs.

Legal counsel: Aid the organization in risk management via proactive counsel.

Strategic planning: Plot a course for the expansion and evolution of Meal Exchange.

Hunger awareness: Manage local and national poverty, hunger, and nutrition information collection and research.

For more information on Meal Exchange at your school, or to learn how to implement the program on your campus, visit www.mealexchange.com.

Volunteer Canada

In December 2002, Volunteer Canada launched www.volunteer.ca. This Web site provides information for volunteers, organizations, and the general public. Here you'll find stats and information on volunteering, and tools for those who already volunteer or would like to start. Volunteer.ca contains a wealth of information, and is funded with support from the federal government.

Keith has never been much of a community activist, but he and the guys from his ball hockey team are Calgary Stampeders volunteers. Each season they assist with promotional events throughout the football games, and throw mini footballs when the Stamps get a touchdown. It's not much work, and they get to watch the game from the sidelines, receive a Stampeders Puma golf shirt, track suit, and winter jacket, and get two seasons passes they can give away to friends and co-workers.

One more thing

You can have a great time on $50 a month, or you can have a great time on $500 a month. Finding time for entertainment should be the hardest thing about having fun, not finding money for it. There are hundreds of ways to relax, enjoy yourself, and have fun, all without blowing your tuition money.

CHAPTER TEN
Sometimes Debt-Free Isn't Worth It

Graduating debt-free isn't possible for every student. And sometimes, it just isn't worth it. Work part-time during the school year, but don't flunk out because you work too much. Don't turn down a summer job that will be your career launching pad because the pay is too low to make tuition. And if your lifelong ambition is to study a program only available at a school you can't afford no matter how much you work, don't give up your goal. This is all about living your dream.

The ultimate goal of graduating with as little debt as possible is to enable you to start your career and life in the strongest position possible. If you have bad credit and high debt, how will you be able to pursue your dreams? When your dream job materializes, but doesn't pay enough for you to keep up with your student loan payments, will you take the higher paying job you hate? Graduating debt-free is hard work, and you have to make hard decisions, but it's worth it. The payoff is the freedom you have after graduation – to take the job you love, to get financing to start your own business, to pursue the career you want.

Keith and I nearly made it through school without any debt. We could have had a smaller wedding, or simply lived together and had the wedding after we graduated. But it was very important to us to get married and move out, and we wanted to share the day with our friends and family, and have a wedding we would be happy with. We felt the debt was worth it, and I don't regret the decision.

Taking out a loan to pay for your education is not a bad investment, if that's what you use the loan for. But when you use loan money to fund weekend ski trips, a nice car, or a killer wardrobe, it's a terrible investment. If you can pay for your tuition, your books, and the bare minimum cost of living without taking out loans, do it!

Sometimes it just won't be possible to get out of school without debt. Your program is long and expensive, your summer job prospects are few, and your spare time to hold a job is non-existent. You may have to get a loan. But hold off as long as possible. Don't just apply for it because everyone does. Loans are your last option, not your first. Have you been Watching Your Money? Have you cut your expenses down in every area? Have you been working full-time in the summer and part-time during the year? Will alternative studying help minimize your costs?

And most importantly, will you be able to handle the debt load once you've graduated? Do you have any job prospects? Will you be able to reach your savings and life goals with a loan payment, as well?

For her first three and a half years of university, Deseree worked thirty hours a week at a part-time job. It meant sometimes taking her books to work, and many all-nighters to fit everything in. "I know that had I not worked as much, I probably would have done better in school. But I did pay my way through school." However, for her last year, Deseree decided she had loftier goals. "For the last year only, I took out a student loan, and worked at volunteer-based jobs that I knew would be awesome on my resume. I lived off government money, and it was the best thing I ever did. I didn't make it out debt-free, but my loan is highly manageable, and in the end it probably helped ensure I got the job I wanted when I finished." Deseree took out loans strategically. She went as long as she could without them, and only took out a loan when it made sense to go into debt based on her career and life goals.

You failed: getting a loan

You've done everything you can to minimize your expenses, and you're still coming up short. It's the last year of school and you want to have more time to enjoy yourself. Or maybe you got into credit card trouble and you couldn't dig yourself out. Whatever your reason, you're turning to loan money to finance your education. It isn't the end of the world. If you've been following the ideas in this book, hopefully you'll be taking out less in loans than most other students will and you'll spend what you do receive wisely. Borrowing money is a fact of life in our society, and money spent on a higher education is definitely a wiser investment than money spent on a new car or television.

But getting a loan isn't easy. There are mountains of paperwork, hours waiting in bank or government offices, and endless hours on the telephone trying to reach someone who can answer your questions. The world of loans is an education in itself.

Types of loans

There are two types of student loans, those funded by the federal government, and those funded by the provincial government. Canada Student Loans are the federally funded loans managed by the National Student Loans Service Centre (NSLSC), except for loans issued before August 1, 2000, which are managed by financial institutions. Provincial loans are funded and managed by each province, which has a student assistance department or office set up (see sidebar for Web sites) to review and approve your application, as well as provide assistance in completing the forms. They actually review and approve your Canada Student Loan, as well – it's one-stop shopping for all your borrowing needs.

Once your application has been approved, the NSLSC steps in, doling out funding, and collecting payments once you've graduated. They will help you create a workable repayment schedule, and if needed, provide assistance with an interest relief or debt reduction program.

Provincial and Territorial Student Assistance Offices

Newfoundland
http://www.edu.gov.nf.ca/studentaid/
Prince Edward Island
http://www.edu.pe.ca/studentloan/resources/index.asp
Nova Scotia
http://studentloans.ednet.ns.ca/
New Brunswick
http://www.studentaid.gnb.ca/
*Quebec
http://www.afe.gouv.qc.ca/Anglais/index.htm
Ontario
http://osap.gov.on.ca
Manitoba
http://www.gov.mb.ca/educate/sfa/pages/sfaFrontDoor_en.html
Saskatchewan
http://www.student-loans.sk.ca/
Alberta
http://www.alis.gov.ab.ca/studentsfinance/main.asp
British Columbia
http://www.aved.gov.bc.ca/studentservices/
Yukon
http://www.gov.yk.ca/depts/education/advanceded/sfahome.html
*Northwest Territories
http://www.nwtsfa.gov.nt.ca/
*Nunavut
http://www.nac.nu.ca/costs/index.html

*Nunavut, the Northwest Territories, and the province of Quebec operate their own student assistance plans. If you are a resident of Nunavut, the Northwest Territories, or Quebec, contact the provincial or territorial Student Assistance Office for further information.

Reality Check: The student loan guidelines I'll talk about in this chapter are for full-time students only, and exclude students with special situations. There are different guidelines and funding limits for part-time students. If you're a parent, an Aboriginal person, or you have a disability or other special situation, different guidelines will apply, and you usually have a better chance at securing not only loans, but also scholarships, grants, and bursaries. Contact your provincial or territorial Student Assistance Office for full details on the criteria for your situation.

Canada Student Loans

The Canada Student Loans guidelines are the same across every province – they are federally subsidized repayable loans. Canada Student Loans will only be provided to a maximum of 60% of your assessed need, up to $165 per week of study. Your application can be submitted anytime after May 1 for the following school year, although applying early will ensure your application is processed quickly. You must reapply for assistance each year.

Eligibility

• You must be a full-time student (60% of a full-time course load)
• You must be enrolled in an approved institution

If you are approved, you'll receive a Notice of Assessment (in some provinces this is sent directly to your school). You'll need to have this signed at your school's financial aid office (bring a book). Once the Notice of Assessment is signed, you must drop it off at a designated Canada Post outlet. The NSLSC will take over, processing your loan and depositing the money into your bank account or sending you a cheque, again depending on your province.

Provincial Student Loans

Provincial student loan guidelines are different for every province. A provincially subsidized repayable loan, the maximum available is 40% of your assessed need, up to $110 per week of study.

If you've done the math, this means that by landing both a federal and a provincial student loan, you can cover 100% of your assessed need. You don't need to apply for the loans separately. The one application is used to assess your need for both federal and provincial assistance.

Eligibility guidelines for provincial student loans can be a little more exclusive. Some or all of the following restrictions may apply. You must:

- be a Canadian citizen or have permanent resident status
- be a resident of the province
- demonstrate that you have financial need
- be enrolled in a minimum of 60% of a full-time course load
- be enrolled in an approved institution
- be enrolled in an approved program
- maintain a certain G.P.A.
- pass a credit check
- have independent student status (see sidebar)

Student loans – the rules of engagement

Each year more than 350,000 students receive Canada Student Loans. But by no means is it an easy process. The application procedure is riddled with confusion, and very frustrating.

Get started early. Application forms are available at your school's financial aid office, at your provincial and territorial Student Assistance Office, and may also be available online. I recommend applying for loans later in your educational program, but once you've made the decision to apply, do it well before you actually need the cash. If you're a first-year student, you don't need to be registered to apply for a student loan, but if you're not accepted, or choose to attend a dif-

All the women, independent...

For most provincial loans, you must identify whether or not you are an independent student, and it affects the amount of loans you will receive. If you are dependent on your parents, you must report their income as well as your own. If you are independent, you must report only your own income (and that of your spouse, or common-law partner, if applicable).

For instance, in New Brunswick, to be considered an independent student, you must meet at least one of the criteria below. You are considered an independent student if you:

- have been out of high school four years
- have been in the work force for two periods of twelve consecutive months and were not a full-time student during this period
- are/were married or common law
- have a dependent living with you
- have no legal guardian/your parents are deceased
- are a permanent ward of a child and family services agency

A student attending school straight out of high school, even if they live in a different province from their parents, is still considered dependent. So if your parents make good money, you probably won't be eligible for a provincial loan, even if they don't plan on giving you any money for school. The rules say they have to, and their income will be a factor in determining your need.

But wait! You're living common-law, so you're independent right? That's not entirely true. You are considered an independent student, but your common-law partner's income must be reported, and it will be considered when they look at your financial resources. Same thing goes for spouses – you have to declare their income.

ferent school than you noted on your application, you need to let them know and may have to complete a new application.

Be honest. Just like your taxes, you could be audited to determine if you were honest on your student loan application. If you do get audited, they'll look for inaccuracies in your statements and if applicable, the information provided by your parents, spouse, or common-law partner. You'll need to provide proof of your expenses – rent receipts, paystubs, etc. If any major inconsistencies are found, even if it was your parents who provided inaccurate information about their income, you're in trouble. Usually it means you won't be eligible for loans, and it could mean you'd immediately have to pay back any loans you received.

The kicker? If your application or file is chosen for an audit, your loan money will be held until the audit is complete, so it's in your best interest to provide the documents they need ASAP. If you don't receive rent receipts on a regular basis, you could be without loan money until your landlord gets back from Cuba and can provide you with them. Always save important receipts for living and school expenses, and proof of income statements.

Pay attention to details. The government is a stickler for details. If you forget to initial one area of your application, or send back an accompanying document, your application could be delayed for months. Ensure you are submitting everything you need to, and that you've crossed your t's and dotted your i's. If you make a mistake on your application, don't erase or white-out the error. Just cross it out and initial the change, like you would on a cheque.

Submit it properly. Once your application is ready to go, you can send it through the mail, drop it off at your provincial or school financial aid office, or you may even be able to complete the application online. After you've submitted your application, wait a week before calling to ensure it has been received properly. You don't want to lose out on a year of tuition because your application was lost in the mail.

Be prepared to appeal. Everyone makes mistakes, so once you receive your Notice of Assessment, review it carefully. If you think you've been wrongly assessed and won't get the money you need, you may have to appeal. The appeal process could take a few weeks or even months, so applying early will give you time to factor this in, if required.

Show me the money!

Each student will receive a different amount of loan money, based on assessed need. Your assessed need is determined by subtracting your resources from your costs. Sounds simple, right? Unfortunately, it's not that easy.

Your costs

Your educational costs and living expenses will be determined both by your program of study and your province of residence. Your allowable educational costs include tuition, books, fees, supplies, and return transportation if you are studying away from home. Your living expenses are not based on your own real expenses. They don't care if you drive a Hummer and only wear Tommy clothing. Instead, you have to follow the Moderate Standard of Living (MSOL) guidelines. The information following is from the 2001 MSOL table.

ALBERTA	
Single student away from home	$747 per month
Single student living at home	$355 per month
SASKATCHEWAN	
Single student away from home	$719 per month
Single student living at home	$346 per month
MANITOBA	
Single student away from home	$768 per month
Single student living at home	$365 per month

ONTARIO	
Single student away from home	$878 per month
Single student living at home	$371 per month
QUEBEC	
Single student away from home	$775 per month
Single student living at home	$373 per month
NEW BRUNSWICK	
Single student away from home	$744 per month
Single student living at home	$328 per month
NOVA SCOTIA	
Single student away from home	$720 per month
Single student living at home	$328 per month
PRINCE EDWARD ISLAND	
Single student away from home	$712 per month
Single student living at home	$322 per month
NEWFOUNDLAND	
Single student away from home	$714 per month
Single student living at home	$330 per month
YUKON	
Single student away from home	$845 per month
Single student living at home	$378 per month
NORTHWEST TERRITORIES	
Single student away from home	$1060 per month
Single student living at home	$413 per month

Your resources

You are required to contribute financially towards your education; however, your required contributions aren't too bad. You'll need to contribute income saved from your pre-study period. If you're going to post-secondary school straight out of high school, that's a ten-week period. If you're a continuing student or adult student, it's an eighteen-week period.

The government expects you to work full-time during this pre-study period and contribute your savings after considering allowable living expenses. The contribution you'll be expected to make from your pre-study period will depend on your income for that time. If you're working for minimum wage, you'll be expected to contribute less than if you were paid a much higher salary. This means you can't party all summer and claim to have no money left afterwards – it won't fly.

If you couldn't find a job that allowed you to save any money beyond your allowable living expenses, or could only work part-time, you'll need to provide proof of your attempts to find a full-time position that would have paid you enough to meet the minimum contribution.

If you choose to work part-time during the school year, this income will be considered; however, according to the government, you are not required to work part-time while attending school.

Don't forget the contributions of your family. As a dependent student, the income of your parents is considered. Their expected financial contribution is based on the number of people in your family, the number of children attending a post-secondary institution, and your family's total income. Again, even if your parents don't give you a single penny, the government is going to pretend they have and will factor that into your budget even if you don't. The contribution of your spouse (married or common-law) is calculated by subtracting the allowable expenses from your annual gross family income. If you have any questions about what you or your family are expected to contribute, see your student aid office right away.

Other financial resources you might have are taken into consideration, as well. This includes bonds, savings or other investments, employment insurance, or scholarships. Again, if you have any questions about what money or assets qualify for inclusion, see your student aid office.

After the government's financial people have determined your assessed need they'll compare this against the maximum assistance limits. Full-time students can receive as much as $275 a week, or $9,350 for a traditional thirty-four-week school year. If your assessed need is less than the maximum, you'll receive your assessed need. If it's more, you're out of luck. You'll receive the maximum and that's it. You cannot be given more than the maximum allowable amount.

> **REALITY CHECK:** If you're applying for assistance before you land a summer job, you may receive a temporary or initial assessment of your expected contribution. This is calculated on the basis of minimum wage for the length of your pre-study period. Once your pre-study period is complete, you'll need to contact the loans office and provide them with statements of your actual earnings for this period. At this point, your expected contribution may change, based on your actual income and expenses. Because you may not receive your final statement of assessed need before tuition is due, you can talk to your student financial aid office for information on how to delay your tuition payment without penalty.

Personal loans, bank loans, and lines of credit

Not every student who needs loans for school decides to go the government route. Leah went to school full-time for three years and part-time for her last year while working full-time. Paying for her tuition was never a problem, but paying for everything else was. "I was lucky to have a grandmother who, upon graduation of high school, offered to pay my tuition costs. I was responsible for all other fees (books, student union fees, transportation, etc.)." Leah worked part-time through the year and full-time during the summer. After her first semester she moved into residence to shorten the commute.

"Living away from home was expensive, and I took out a student line of credit to finance it. When I finished my degree I had approximately $14,000 on my line of credit. The majority of my line of credit went to pay fees for residence, some went towards a computer, and the rest to other living expenses and school fees." While Leah paid a few hundred dollars extra in interest on the line of credit than she would have with a student loan, she feels it was worth it as it kept her from treating the money as free.

"The absolute smartest thing I did in terms of debt was to get a line of credit instead of pushing for a government loan. I think that I gained financial responsibility because I received a monthly statement and I had to pay interest monthly instead of receiving it at the end of school. I knew where my money was going and it was my responsibility to ensure I managed it properly. I had some bumps when I shopped more than I should have, but I feel I gained responsibility because of those bumps. I saw friends who had government loans who didn't know what money they would get from their loan after working for the summer, didn't have the monthly reminders of their debt, and didn't show financial responsibility when it mattered. My only advice to students would be to take control of your debt early in your university career. If you have to finance through loans, be sure to keep a reminder of what those loans and interest are so you aren't as inclined to mismanage the funds."

You might choose a non-government loan for personal reasons, or because you don't qualify for a government loan. There are three non-government loans – personal, bank, or line of credit.

Personal loan

A personal loan is a loan someone personally gives you, not a bank. It might be a wealthy relative or family friend, someone who will lend you money when you need it, as a loan, not as a gift. Be very careful in this situation, though. Write down all the terms of your agreement, including interest. And stick to them. There's nothing that will sour a relationship faster than a disagreement over money. And if someone is offering to lend you money, recognize and appreciate the offer. They'll probably make much less interest off of you than they could have investing somewhere else.

Bank loan

A bank loan is just that, a loan from a bank. You'll get a set amount, and you'll start owing interest and principal payments right away. Shop around for the best rates. Try credit unions and other non-traditional financial institutions, but avoid the loan shark, payday kinds of places as their interest rates and fees are through the roof. Most banks have special loans for students, and will require a co-signer – your spouse, parents, or another individual. Some students use bank loans as a way to pay tuition on a monthly basis. By the time the next fall rolls around, the past year's tuition loan is paid, and it's time for another.

Line of credit

A line of credit is basically a flexible loan. You are approved for a specific limit, like $5,000. You can then take out money when you need it, and only owe interest on the amount you've used. Most student lines of credit allow you to pay only the interest while you're still in school, and you might not have to start paying back the principal until up to six months after graduation.

Emergency loans

Your student loan money may not arrive in time to pay your bills. What do you do when you're flat broke and don't expect a cheque for another few weeks? There is help available. Most schools have an emergency fund to help students facing cash crunches. If your bank account is getting low and you're not sure where your grocery money is going to come from, don't wait until the last second. Visit the financial services office and talk to an advisor. You may be approved for an emergency loan to cover your short-term need. If your situation is really bad, the emergency money may be designated as a grant, and you won't have to repay it. Talk to someone in the financial services office – these programs aren't usually publicized, and only they will have the details about what's available to you.

Paying it back, and then some

Six months after you leave your studies (whether you graduated, failed, got kicked out, or for any other reason), you are required to begin repaying your loan, with interest. You must make contact with your loan provider to discuss the terms of the repayment.

While the government covered the interest on your loan during your time in school, you're on the hook for it now. Interest on student loans is generally prime rate plus a percentage point or two, so depending on interest rates when it comes time to pay back your loans, you could be paying a steep price. Interest paid on student loans is tax deductible, but you don't get back all that money, just a small portion of it.

Here's an example. For a student loan of $5,000, with an interest rate of 8% and a repayment target of four years, once your term is up you'll have actually paid $5859.10. An interest rate jump to 10% means you'll pay $6,087.02. Need a bigger loan? Let's say you took $10,000 in loan money, and you're planning on paying it off over nine years, the standard repayment schedule. At 10% interest, once you're done paying, you'll actually have paid $15,204.98. Basic math dictates that the faster you can pay off your student loans, the better. And yes, I got help with that calculation.

Did you know that you could negotiate a lower student loan interest rate? All you have to do is ask and they may just drop a percentage point or two. If they won't drop the rate and you think it's too high, you might consider getting a second loan, one with a lower interest rate, and paying off your student loan with the second one. For instance, ING Direct offers a line of credit with interest rates as low as 6.2%. Just remember, the interest paid on a student loan is tax deductible, so talk to a financial planner to see what's right for you.

Can't make your payments? You don't have to move to another province and forget to leave a forwarding address. There is assistance in place to help you during tough times.

Interest Relief (IR) is available for both federal and provincial student loans. If your income is low enough that payments are an undue hardship, you may be eligible for IR. You apply through your loan provider, and the federal and provincial governments will pay the interest on the loans. IR is approved for six months at a time, and you can continue to reapply every six months until assistance is no longer required. In 2000/2001, 154,895 borrowers received assistance from this program. That number's important. It means that 154,895 graduates did not find jobs that paid well enough for them to manage their debt payments without assistance.

The Debt Reduction in Repayment program (DRR) is available for both federal and provincial student loans. You can apply for this program through your loan provider, and if approved, your debt will be reduced. There are conditions. Your loan payments must exceed a given percentage of your income, you must have exhausted Interest Relief, and five years must have passed since you completed your studies. The maximum reduction allowed is $10,000 or 50% of the principal of your Canada Student Loan, whichever is less. For your provincial student loan, the maximum reduction allowed is $4,000 or 50% of the principal, whichever is less. As with all government initiatives, if it sounds too good to be true, it probably is. The DRR assisted just 614 students in 2000/2001.

Maintenance

You may start receiving student loans while in your first, second, or subsequent years of study. Because you don't have to begin paying your loans or the interest on them until you finish school, it's important that you let the loans people know you're still a student. Some students assume this is automatic, and it's not. If you continue your studies as a full-time student, you need to confirm this to ensure you maintain your interest-free status. If you enrol as a part-time student, you'll be required to pay only the interest portion of your loan repayment while studying part-time.

You've only got six months from the end of your last period of study to confirm your continued enrolment. Let the NSLSC or your bank (if the loan is with them) know about your status as soon as you have it confirmed with the school. Forget to confirm your continued enrolment and you'll be expected to start replaying your loans.

I did say you don't have to move to another province and not leave a forwarding address to avoid paying your student loan back. Actually, doing so will get you in a lot of hot water. When they're done school and the first loan payment comes due, often students have moved from the place they lived during school. Unfortunately, many students forget to notify the National Student Loans Service Centre.

If you haven't given them your change of address, the NSLSC will send you a letter saying you owe them the first payment on your loans. You don't get the letter, and you don't make a payment. Now, if this were a bank loan you didn't make a payment on, the bank would hunt you down and harass you. But the NSLSC doesn't do that – they expect you to contact them. If you don't get in touch with them to work out your repayment terms and you don't make a payment for three months, you've defaulted on your loan. This will be reported on your credit file, so don't wait for them to call you. As soon as you have your diploma, degree, or certificate in hand, give them a call and set up your payment plan. You can arrange for automatic withdrawals from your bank account that will begin when those six grace months are up.

No job, no money

For all your hard work and effort, you may not get a job when you graduate, or it may not pay enough to make your minimum debt payments and cover the cost of living. This might not have anything to do with your skills, your intelligence, or your personality. It's just a reality of today's world that the ideal job is not always waiting for us the day we graduate. It might mean taking a job you don't like, or one that is beneath your normal standards. It might mean moving back home with your parents, or applying for social assistance. Whatever your decision, make sure it is proactive. One of the biggest mistakes graduates make is trying to ignore their financial situation.

You have to face reality. Lots of people are afraid to balance their chequebook, to create a Watching Your Money type of plan, or to talk with their creditors. It may seem easier just to try to ignore the problem, ignore the phone calls from collection agencies, and ignore your increasing credit card balance. But you have an education, and you're way too smart to go down this path.

An amazing amount of problems can be resolved just by sitting down with your banker or a financial planner. You'll get a clear picture of where you stand financially, how your credit is being affected, and what you can do to turn things around.

For years, students would rack up major student loans and a few months after graduation declare bankruptcy. Sure, it destroyed their credit, but it also got them out of a $40,000 debt. But the government soon wised up to this practice and these days declaring bankruptcy isn't something you can just do to avoid paying back your student loans. If student loan debt is one of your major debts, bankruptcy won't help you. You must be out of school for at least ten years before student loan debts will be erased by bankruptcy.

Consolidation order

If you financed your education through loans, credit cards, or other consumer credit and you're in over your head, you might be able to avoid bankruptcy by meeting with your creditors, attending credit counselling, taking out a debt consolidation loan, or, depending on your province, applying for a consolidation order. A consolidation order sets out the amount and the times when payments are due to the court. The court will distribute your payments to your creditors over a period of three years, which frees you from creditor harassment and wage garnishment. You do not lose your assets.

Consumer proposal

You could also try a consumer proposal. Under the *Bankruptcy and Insolvency Act* you may make a proposal to your creditors to reduce the amount of your debts, extend the time you have to pay off the debt, or provide some combination of both. Until your consumer proposal is withdrawn, rejected, or otherwise ended, your creditors cannot try to recover their debts outside of the program.

Let's say you owe $10,000 to Visa, and your minimum monthly payment is $250. Using the consumer proposal, you can propose that you will pay $150 each month until the debt is paid. You can also propose that you will only pay back $7,000 of the debt, and the interest may be reduced. While this may seem like an easy way to avoid paying your bills, it's not. Although you'll get some help from the government, there is a mountain of paperwork you'll need to complete, and it isn't free. Also, creditors do not have to accept the proposal. If the proposal is rejected, it's open season on your assets and wages again.

Bankruptcy

Bankruptcy is your last resort. Everything you own, except a few items, will be sold and the money raised will go to your creditors. Your debts will be erased, and your creditors are not allowed to contact or harass you. Watch out, though. If you declare bankruptcy but one of your debts was co-signed, your co-signer is now responsible for that debt – it isn't removed.

Your credit report will show your bankruptcy for anywhere from six to fourteen years, depending on your province and any previous bankruptcies. With this on your report, you'll have a hard time getting a mortgage, credit card, loan, or even a cell phone. You may even be denied a job. Financial institutions and other companies that require employees be bonded will generally not hire you if you have a bankruptcy on file.

Going bankrupt isn't free, either. You'll owe $1,000 or more to the bankruptcy trustee, and this isn't absolved by the bankruptcy. So once you're out of debt by bankruptcy, you're right back in it again. Sounds like a government plan to me, all right.

SINK OR SWIM

One more thing

I included loan information in the last chapter of this book for a reason. There are so many creative and proactive things you can do first to fund your education before turning to borrowed money. Know your breaking point. Understand when the time has honestly come for you to apply for loans to finish your education. Drop out of school because you hate the program, you want to try something else, or you have a once in a lifetime chance to tour with the Cirque du Soleil, but don't ever drop out because you can't afford it. You have so many resources at your disposal, and you'll always regret the decision to end your education.

CHAPTER ELEVEN
You Made it This Far

So, this is the end. I hope I've provided you with some strategies and ideas to make getting your degree, diploma, or certificate easier.

The majority of non-students cite financial concerns as the number one reason why they didn't attend a post-secondary institution. But an education is within anyone's reach. It's all about the decisions you make. Choosing a program, finding a place to live, limiting your spending, and valuing your financial future are decisions that will determine your future.

Giving back

When I graduated from high school, I didn't have many resources for post-secondary school. My parents did what they could, and I know they wished they could do more. My mom let me live at home, and my dad continued to pay child support to help her with the expenses, although legally he didn't have to, as I was eighteen. I knew they were giving what they could, and I appreciated it.

Throughout high school I made extra spending money babysitting for the children of my mom's friends, a group we called "the Martimers" as they were all originally from back east, but worked and raised their families in Calgary. One of the Maritimers, Susan, was a very close friend of our family and had helped us get on our feet when we first moved to the city. Susan threw me a graduation party, and all the Maritimers were there. After the cake was cut, Susan brought out the gifts – a dozen envelopes. Instead of buying presents, Susan had asked each person to write a cheque that I could use for tuition. The generosity of these family friends was amazing. I had enough money to pay for an entire semester of university. I didn't know what to say.

Now that I am working full-time, I could afford to pay back the money to those friends, but that's not what they'd want. Instead, I'm going to help others with their education. It's kind of like that movie, *Pay it Forward*, and now it's my turn to do a student a favour.

You can give back in many ways. At Christmastime, I give money to the campus food bank. While I never used their services, thousands of students across Canada depend on their campus food banks to ensure they aren't eating Mr. Noodle for weeks on end. When you graduate and begin making money, remember to support those students who are still struggling. Give to the campus food bank or to another campus support service.

One of the issues I touched on briefly is that once you graduate, the plight of students is no longer your problem. Supporting your alumni association is one way to remind yourself that the need exists – the same need you once felt. At some schools alumni associations exist only to keep track of graduates, hold events, and communicate news. At others, however, the alumni association is an integral part of the school, providing funding for a variety of causes. For instance, at Lakehead University in Thunder Bay, alumni contributions are used to provide aid to students, improvements to the library holding, new equipment, assistance to varsity sports, and help to attract and retain academic talent.

I want to hear from you!

When I began writing this book, a lot of people told me, "I can't wait to read it, my kid/friend/brother/girlfriend is having a hard time paying for school, and this would be a great book for them."

So now that you're at the end of this book, I'd like to hear from you. Which suggestions were helpful? Which ones weren't? What have you done to achieve your goals? What has been your motivation? Have I provided useful advice or inspiration?

As I write this, post-secondary education in Canada is facing major challenges. One of these challenges is differential tuition, now being reviewed by my alma mater. Differential tuition would charge students different tuition based on their faculty. It's unclear whether the tuition would be based on the actual cost of running the faculty, or the amount of corporate support a faculty could get. While many technical schools and colleges have dealt with differential tuition for years, it's comparatively revolutionary for universities. Whatever happens, it will alter the educational playing field yet again.

This book wouldn't have been possible without the input of students and graduates across Canada. I encourage you to send me your stories – the successes, the failures, and your suggestions and advice for a future edition of *Sink or Swim: Get Your Degree Without Drowning in Debt.*

Visit www.sarahdeveau.com to send me your feedback, or e-mail me at feedback@sarahdeveau.com. Good luck!

BIBLIOGRAPHY

Books

Duguay, Dara. *Don't Spend Your Raise: and 59 Other Money Rules You Can't Afford to Break.* Contemporary Books Inc, 2003.

Mladen, Caryn, David Rosen and Pat Ordovensky. *University Planning for Dummies for Canadians.* Macmillan Canada, 2001.

Yate, Martin. *Resumes that Knock 'Em Dead.* Adams Media Corporation, 2002.

Yate, Martin. *Cover Letters that Knock 'Em Dead.* Adams Media Corporation, 2002.

Dacyczyn, Amy. *The Complete Tightwad Gazette.* Villard, 1998.

Begoun, Paula. *Don't Go to the Cosmetics Counter Without Me.* Beginning Press, 2003.

Articles

Caspar, John. *Five Ways to Save Money.*
http://money.msn.ca/articles/banking/commentary/P391042.asp

Hwang, Justine. *Living with Your Parents (without going crazy).*
http://www.iamnext.com/people/tips/parents.html

Websites

Adbusters: http://www.adbusters.org

ACNielson: http://www.acnielsen.com

AirMiles: http://www.airmiles.ca

Alberta Learning Information Service: http://alis.gov.ab.ca/studentsfinance/main.asp

All Recipes: http://www.allrecipes.com

As Prime Minister Awards: http://www.asprimeminister.com

Bankruptcy and Insolvency Act: http://laws.justice.gc.ca

British Columbia Student Financial Aid: http://www.aved.gov.bc.ca/studentservices

Business Development Bank of Canada: http://www.bdc.ca

Buy Nothing Christmas: http://www.buynothingchristmas.org

Canada Job Bank: http://www.jobbank.gc.ca

Canada-Saskatchewan Integrated Student Loans Program: http://www.student-loans.sk.ca

Canadian Automobile Association: http://www.caa.ca

Canadian Free Stuff: http://www.canadianfreestuff.com

Canadian Youth Business Foundation: http://www.youthbusiness.com

CanLearn Interactive: http://www.canlearn.ca

Canuck Cash: http://www.canuckcash.ca

Check Mark Inc.: http://www.checkmarkinc.com

Dollar Stretcher: http://www.dollarstretcher.com

Edge: http://edgeip.com

FinAid! The SmartStudent Guide to Financial Aid: http://www.finaid.org

Lakehead University: http://www.lakeheadu.ca

Manitoba Student Aid: http://gov.mb.ca/educate/sfa/pages/sfaFrontDoor_en.html

Meal Exchange: http://www.mealexchange.com

Millennium Scholarship Foundation: http://www.millenniumscholarships.ca

New Brunswick Student Financial Services: http://www.studentaid.gnb.ca

Newfoundland Student Financial Services: http://www.edu.gov.nf.ca/studentaid

Northwest Territories Student Financial Assistance:
http://nwtsfa.gov.nt.ca
Nova Scotia Student Assistance: http://studentloans.ednet.ns.ca
Nunavut Arctic College: http://www.nac.nu.ca
Ontario Student Assistance Program: http://osap.gov.on.ca
Prince Edward Island Student Financial Services:
http://www.edu.pe.ca/studentloan/guide
Quebec Student Assistance: http://www.afe.gouv.qc.ca/index.htm
Rapid Chek Reporting, Inc.: http://www.rapidchek.com
Roommate Service: http://www.roomateservice.com
Scholarship Canada: http://www.scholarshipscanada.com
School Finder: http://schoolfinder.com
Sensor Quality Management: http://www.sqm.ca
Shop 'n Chek Worldwide: http://www.shopnchek.com
Student Awards: http://www.studentawards.com
The Corporate Research Group: http://www.thecrg.com
Totally Free Canadian Stuff:
geocities.com/totallyfreecanadianstuff/index.html
Transport Canada: http://www.tc.gc.ca
Travel CUTS Student Work Abroad Program: http://www.swap.ca
University of Calgary: http://www.ucalgary.ca
University of Manitoba: http://www.umanitoba.ca
University of Saskatchewan: http://www.usask.ca
Volunteer Canada: http://www.volunteer.ca
Yukon Student Financial Assistance: http://www.gov.yk.ca/depts/education/advanceded/sfa/index.html